Metamorphosis

How Jesus of Nazareth
Vanquished the Legion of Fear

Russell M. Lawson

WIPF & STOCK · Eugene, Oregon

Wipf and Stock Publishers
199 W 8th Ave, Suite 3
Eugene, OR 97401

Metamorphosis
How Jesus of Nazareth Vanquished the Legion of Fear
By Lawson, Russell M.
Copyright©2019 by Lawson, Russell M.
ISBN 13: 978-1-5326-9471-4
Publication date 6/20/2019
Previously published by St. Polycarp Publishing House, 2019

For Riley

For God hath not given us the spirit of fear, but of power, and of love, and of a sound mind.

2 Timothy 1:7

CONTENTS

Preface   ix

PART I
THE LEGION OF FEAR
1. Legion   3
2. An Age of Fear   11
3. The Terror of Nature and the Divine   21
4. An Age of Deception   37

PART II
THE TRANSCENDENT
5. A Vision of the Night   47
6. Astral Beckoning   59
7. Pondering   65
8. A Child is Born   71
9. Hidden Years   77
10. Deceiver   85

PART III
TRANSFIGURATION
11. Timeless Enters Time   95
12. Metamorphosis   105
13. The Healer   111
14. The Teacher   119
15. Son of Man   135
16. Truth   155

PART IV
THE LEGION OF FEAR VANQUISHED
17. The Continuing Presence of Fear   165
18. The Voice of a Child   171
19. I Am   181
20. The Gospel of the Absurd   189

21. Perfect Love — 193

Notes — 197
Sources Consulted — 201
About the Author — 207

PREFACE

This book is the culmination of many years spent addressing two questions: Why did Christ come when He did? And what happened as a result? The first question has exercised the minds of countless theologians, philosophers, and historians, those who assume through faith that the Son of God could determine whence He appeared among humans. Why during the Roman Empire? Why during the reign of Herod the Great or his successor Herod Archelaus? Why not centuries earlier, or centuries later? Why at this particular time, two thousand years ago? Such answers as have been proposed—that He arrived as the Messiah to fulfill God's promise to the Jews; that He arrived when the *Pax Romana* provided the stability and continuity necessary for the spread of Christianity throughout the Mediterranean region; that He arrived when humans needed Him most—are sufficient, if not wholly satisfactory, answers to the question. One way to approach the question, *Why did Christ come when He did?*, is to ask the corollary, *And what happened as a result?*, which provides a host of new possibilities. He came to establish the Church; He came to replace the Old Testament

Law, the old covenant, with a new covenant; He came to inaugurate the Great Commission, to spread His Word throughout the world; He came to save the world; He inaugurated the greatest revolution in thought, culture, and society, the world has ever seen before and since. Which one is true? What is the answer?

Contemplating these questions for many years from the perspective of a human living in time two thousand years after the fact, wondering about the impact of Christ on humans in the past and today, reflecting on the impact of the Incarnation on my own life, during which fear has played a huge part, I have derived an interpretation of the significance of Christ based on history, scripture, philosophy, and personal experience.

My premise is that all humans, living in time, are overwhelmed by fear, an extreme example being that experienced by the Gerasene Demoniac. The *legion of fear* dominates human existence and can be explored historically and philosophically. Part 1 of the book examines the overwhelming fear that controlled humans at the time of the Incarnation. It begins with the story of Legion of Gerasa, followed by chapters examining how humans at this time struggled against nature, other humans, and the divine, so that the legion of fear was triumphant. Part 2 evokes how the timeless entered time by means of the Incarnation, which led to a transformation, as explained in Part 3, not only to the Gerasene Demoniac but also in the struggle of humans against nature, other humans, and the divine. A metamorphosis occurred, and Part 4 explains how Christ vanquishes the legion of fear through love.

I

THE LEGION OF FEAR

In the ancient world, nothing could stop fear and its consequences. Fear of the natural environment: storms on land and sea, famine, disease, and death; fear of other humans who hurt, fight, steal, humiliate, destroy, kill; fear of the divine: jealous gods, wrathful gods, distant gods, unknown gods. From the beginning to the end of life, people lived in time, and feared what time brought. They yearned for answers to the manifold questions of life, sought the presence of God in so many ways, looked for the healing presence of the divine. Many people in the ancient world felt that they found the answer. But the answer, the solution to the problem of fear, was elusive.

1

LEGION

Fear filled him. Fear had attached itself to his very being. It was a presence, something a part of him, deep inside, usually hidden, absent from awareness.

All creatures in each moment sense *the Fear*. Instinct usually takes over to impel the creature to act, to survive, to put off, for a time, the inevitable. Humans sense *the Fear* but willingly brush it aside, submerge it, ignore it, make it appear ludicrous, mask it. But it is unrelenting. *The Fear* arrives from everywhere, nowhere, instantly surrounding its prey, overwhelming, suffocating.

The Fear is the most horrible nightmare, the most disgusting creature that attacks without warning, its coils, or pincers, or tentacles grab, overpower, squeeze, cut, tear the flesh, wrap around the throat, strangling, excruciating.

The Fear strikes, a plague, erupting with horrible swelling boils, aching, bulging with pus, sickening, bringing about a slow agonizing end to life. *Fear* has a tendency to reproduce, like a virus splitting, dividing, becoming infinitesimal in number, *legion*, finding obscure parts of the brain to hide and wait for a moment of weakness in the host at which time to emerge, attack, disable.

The Fear invaded a man.

The Fear was the most hideous torture, burning the man alive at the stake of thoughts and emotions, drowning him slowly in his past guilt and sin, nailing him to the cross of the mistakes of all humankind and forcing him to bleed, suffocate, and thirst to death.

The Fear was his dark side, always on the brink of taking over his mind. In each moment, the fear convinced him that he would lose control, give in to the obsessions, do exactly what he did not want to do. To become something different, unrecognizable. To become *Legion*.

Thousands of images, experiences, memories, feelings of guilt and humiliation, times of wanting to do something but being afraid to do it, moments of embarrassment and inaction, other times of action that were wrong, sinful: These were *legion*, stored in his mind, penetrating every aspect of the present, like countless atoms banging against the walls of his brain, wishing to exit, to be free—but *the Fear* kept them in control, waiting for the right time, the exact moment—*when* the man never knew—and without warning the legion odemons, of the images of the past, would come together, marshaled under the commanding Fear, and the man then would be faced with images of committing the unthinkable.

He thought of the most disgusting things, the most horrible crimes, the excruciating details of murder, all a product of his ruminating mind. He was like a cow, a horse, a donkey, an ass, grazing, hungering for grass, and more grass, unable to fill himself, unable to stop, obsessed with eating, compulsively swallowing—but it was never enough.

The thought, the panic, gripped him, as images, a legion of images, erupted in his consciousness about death and destruction and evil and sorrow. His future appeared determined. Fantastic thoughts foretold reality.

He was a demon, an agent of Hell, intent on destruction, on murder, biding his time, awaiting the moment when suddenly he would lose all sanity, all control, and he would throttle, strangle, and his victim would die horribly without a sound, silently.

The webs of fear were spun in earlier years. To live is to experience fear. The man's fear was in response to the uncertainty of his environment—the constant possibility of loneliness, the darkness of night, the unknown, pain. The Fear was the result of restlessness, the dependence on the passing moment, as well as the narcissistic search for constant gratification, for pleasure to counter the pain of existence. Anecdotal teachings of the past support the reliance upon doubts and fears to guide humans through the years; messages of despair and unhappiness seep into the brains of old and young alike, instilling an infernal hubris and arrogance, that what cannot be known for sure is not worth knowing, indeed does not exist. Decay overwhelms delight and joy. Pleasure, beauty, and euphoria give way to pain, blemishes, and sorrow.

The man was a certain person in a certain place in a certain time who represented all humans in all places and in all times. Ancient sources briefly describe the man tortured by fear. He is unnamed save for his own appellation: *Legion*.

Whatever creature inhabited his brain, whatever *legion* of demons possessed his soul—it stirred the pot of fantasy with so many ingredients of fear and foreboding, so many tormented images of crime, of uncontrollable sins, insane murders, followed by accusations, torture, dungeon, chains, trial, confession, guilt, execution.

The Fear became the dominating force in his life. Every morning upon awakening his mind ferreted within to find a thought, an obsession, with which to destroy his sense of peace, his happiness. The legion of images flocked about him, settled upon him, determining the day of fear and anxiety. He could not rid himself of the thoughts that entered his consciousness; he could not reason them away; he could not convince himself that he would not do what he imagined. The Fear was like a great automaton within him, calculating, indiscriminate, unpredictable, and completely autonomous from what this man, Legion, wanted, wished, thought, or said.

He was unable sometimes to think because of the overwhelming presence of *the Fear*, his mind jumbled by so many images of disaster and despair—unspeakable images that he could not believe he was having, and yet he was. They were images of folly, one after the other. He dreamed of murder, of patricide, of random death, of rape and torture, involving people known and unknown. He envisioned himself as the agent of destruction. The resultant guilt mixed with confusion of how to explain it, what to do about it. So random were the fantasies that they were ultimately nonsensical.

Legion tried everything he could think of to resist, to fight, to avoid, to ignore; to embrace fear so to familiarize himself with it, to laugh at it. Nothing worked. Only death would bring it to an end. But death is not an option for a person unwilling to die. Death is to be resisted. Every part of one's being—mind, body, spirit—must fight to survive.

Resist. Resist the foe. Resist the fear. Struggle against it. Force it away. Throttle it. Destroy it. Murder it. Free yourself from it at all costs. Run from it.

Legion had tried running from fear time and again. When the thoughts came, he tried to stifle the fear by going outside into the summer heat or cool winter nights; he drank wine beyond normal intoxication; he had sex, thought of sex; he hid in places of darkness to see if the Fear would go away; he called out to Heaven for help; he tried hiding in the city, anonymous, normal; he tried secluding himself. Fruitless. Winless. Exhausted.

How does a person resist *Fear*? How does a person resist the countless images from the past of error, sin, wretchedness, lust, violence? How is a random thought, a sensation, an image, a horrible feeling in the pit of the stomach, the stark loneliness, the seclusion from reality, the temptation, the deception, the demonization of the mind, the overwhelming presence of a legion of fear—how is it to be resisted?

Legion's entire life had been focused on resisting. He had resisted how he looked, who he was, what he was taught, how he lived, where he lived, his society, his culture, dominant institutions, religious leaders, education, teachers, morals, ethics, government, war, life, death, and the present. He resisted anything that tried to pigeon-hole him, to define him, to control him, to institutionalize him, to make him what he was not.

To spend a life resisting yields questions upon questions. Some questions are simple, childlike: *Why do we steal? Why do we lust for another? Why do we lie? Why do we seek to hurt? Why are we only concerned with Self?* Some questions are profound, unknowable: *How can the diversity of nature have a single point of origin? How can the years and months of countless centuries have a representative moment? How can the multitude be singular? How can the lives and thoughts of humans throughout time be contained in one?* Then there were the ultimate unanswerable questions: *Is there a god or gods? Who? What does he, they, want from us? Why does he, they, allow chaos, destruction, war, disease, hunger, death? What deity/deities would allow the suffering seen everywhere, every day, throughout time? What deity/deities would allow such Fear?*

Legion personified the age-old struggle between freedom and order, liberty and authority. The liberty and freedoms human yearn for are opposed by the restrictions of society, artificial rules that impede natural inclinations, systems that guarantee order in a world filled with potential chaos. Youthful ideas of wantonness and misbehavior are confronted by authority imposing restrictions and regulations. The ways of the body, feeling, going against the ways of the mind, thought. Legion's fantasy world—some of it he allowed, some of it he could not help—was opposed by the standards, norms, and decorum of society.

His fears were a veritable army of images, thoughts, recollections, fantasies, and dreams covering years of angst about physical cowardice, angst about self-control and obsessive thoughts, guilt about so many actions based on fantasy and images. He had obsessed about making mistakes, saying the wrong thing, looking askance at a person, appearing ridiculous, obsessing over the erotic. He had legions of guilt over lusting after women in his heart. There were legions of women whom he had never touched, spoken to, even met. They were in his mind. They were the Sirens, and Jezebel, and Helen, and every exotic dancer, and adulterer, and prostitute: hundreds, thousands, millions—all available to fantasize about, with whom to commit adultery in the heart. He was like David peering at Bathsheba, then taking her again and again. Legion had done this so many times, countless times; there had been one Bathsheba after another, one for each moment, each second, and his mind had been dazzled by beauty, sexuality, eroticism, such that he had been unable to think, to analyze, but only had to have more, and more, insatiable, unrelenting. He was like Solomon with his hundreds of concubines, one for every day of the year—and more. Solomon's concubines represented all women Legion had ever seen, the thousands he had fantasized about, if but for an instant, a second, when glancing at a person walking by, or thinking randomly of a great imaginary beauty, instantaneously taking in her form, her eyes, her lips, her hair, her smile, and instantaneously taking her, making love to her, fulfilling his lust through her. Thousands upon thousands of times, all packed in his mind, the many legions of beauties. He had like Paul, a thorn in his flesh, a thorn that also plagued Augustine, who was unable to break from his obsession over the erotic. To live and deal with the uncertainty of the moment, the lack of pleasure, the lack of excitement, the mind can bring forth an encyclopedia of pleasurable thoughts based on memory and perception. And in the moment, images and thoughts dominate, control, scintillate, and one becomes like a savage, an erotic untamed savage hungry for sex and pleasure. But then the instant passes, the moment is gone, the illusion vanishes, the image disappears, and Legion was alone, just himself.

He was insane with guilt, grief, and fear. Guilt is a deep well in the human psyche, and it takes much effort to descend deeper and deeper into the well of the past to discover the pangs of conscience that represent guilt. His guilt combined with poor self-esteem and an appalling lack of confidence; it burdened him with chains of the weight of the past.

He was known throughout the region as a man in chains, naked and savage, violent and angry, fearsome, haunting. He was a man pursued. All throughout the village. Everywhere. No place to hide. Who were the pursers? Legion did not know. Likewise, he did not know what they wanted, why he was being pursued. He kept trying to hide. He found the best place of refuge to be living among the tombs of the dead.

Humans, content to live among themselves in their artificial habitats of villages, towns, and cities, eschew the wild and savage, places of filth, environments that are tainted by death and suffering. No one would willingly choose to live among tombs of the dead—a graveyard—any more than one would choose to associate with swine and their filthy pens. But this is precisely where Legion lived, in a graveyard adjoining a herd of swine. Here he could remain untouched by his fellow humans, who dared not join such a person in such a dismal and disgusting place.

2

AN AGE OF FEAR

The Greek philosopher and author of *Lives* Plutarch, one of the first essayists in world history, continually challenged his contemporaries of the first century, *Anno Domini*, with writings of wit and perspicuity. In one essay, *On the Use of Reason by Irrational Animals*, Plutarch imagined a scene taken from the characters and setting of the *Odyssey* when the witch Circe has kidnapped Odysseus's men and metamorphosed them into swine. Odysseus, considered by Homer as the most intelligent of the Greeks of his time, in attempting to free his men is confronted by one of his crew-turned-swine, who calls himself Grunter (Gryllus). Grunter engages in a debate with wise Odysseus, arguing that the lot of a pig is preferable to the lot of humans. He argues that pigs, like all animals, since they do not concern themselves with time, live day to day, and have little to fear, save death, which all corporeal beings experience. Further, Grunter says persuasively that animals, even pigs, have a natural courage, which humans lack—convention, laws, and societal expectations force humans to live in fear that their actions will contradict what other humans expect. Every moment a human considers what will be the consequence of his/her action; once the action has occurred, the human constantly reassesses what he/she has done, and whether or not others will accept or criticize. Fear of possible criticism overwhelms the day-to-day lives of humans. But what does a pig, living in sloth, have to fear from his fellows?

What humans did and thought overwhelmed Legion, who was not alone in his suffering among the people of his time and place, when Herod the Great and his successors ruled. Humans at this time had been unable to break from the constant cycle of pain, mental and physical anguish, oppression, conflict, poverty, and the overwhelming fear that accompanied such maladies. This was an age of fear.

The fear manifested itself in Legion's time in so many ways. There were thousands of real and imaginary fears. Men, women, children, young and old, sick and healthy, rich and poor, feared the consequences of living in a natural world where life was frequently short and came to an end quickly and violently. Humans of the time were subject to unforeseen debilitating illnesses, especially the horror of leprosy, which disfigured and drove a person senseless as it slowly killed. And there was no cure. As bad was the threat of starvation: famine was just around the corner in the ancient world, even during times of plenty. Weather was never predictable: one year drought followed by another of rains and flooding. Plagues of varying kinds gripped the land, stripped crops, weakened animals, destroyed life. Humans from the beginning had plagued themselves with violence, conflict, and war, all of which occupied the mind, overwhelmed the senses, and resulted in a universal fear: among fighters and victims, victors and vanquished, alike. How great was the hand of God in human suffering? Was it divine will that drove people to kill? that caused war and the destruction of the innocent? Who allowed the enslavement of countless women and children? Who brought plagues upon the people? Who struck the healthy with illness? Who caused the suffering of the mortally ill? What has been God's purpose? What could, can, humans do to change, or at least accommodate and prepare for, the mysterious ways of God?

These questions overwhelmed Legion, as they did so many others, Gentiles and Jews who two thousand years ago lived in the region between the eastern Mediterranean and the Tigris and Euphrates rivers valleys. Like most places in world history, peoples of this region, the *Levant*, spent their years fighting and dying for rights of land, water, and trade; for the various divinities associated with rivers, mountains, and plains; and for the whims of warlords and kings. Legion lived in a region called *Decapolis* by his contemporaries: ten independent cities east of the Sea of Galilee. Ancient geographers were not always in agreement about the names, and even numbers, of the cities of Decapolis. The Elder Pliny (*Natural History*, 5:16) described Decapolis as including Damascus (which was northeast of the Sea of Galilee), Scythopolis (west of the Jordan River), Philadelphia, Canatha, Hippo, Dion, Rhaphana, Pella, Gadara, and Galasa (Gerasa). Legion was from the town of Gerasa, which lay on the eastern shores of the Sea of Galilee.

The Sea of Galilee was a lake formed by the Jordan River; it went by several names, such as Lake Tiberius, named for the Roman city at its western shores, the namesake of the Emperor; Gennesaret, the name of a town and region on its northwestern shore; and Chinnereth, a Hebrew appellation, "harp-shaped," which denoted the shape of the lake, more long than wide, and bulging on its western side, where the shores washed plains descending from surrounding hills, as opposed to the eastern shores, which were much steeper, hence fewer towns. The Sea of

Galilee and Jordan Valley centered a plentiful land of rich vegetation, well-watered, the fruits of which fed the thousands of people of numerous villages inhabited by shopkeepers, artisans, agriculturalists, and fishers. Families whose lives depended on the Sea of Galilee lived in the many towns along the shores. The water was fresh and good tasting and the fish were prolific

Although a freshwater lake of modest size—thirteen miles at its greatest extent—the mountainous landscape surrounding the lake, which was below sea level, led to frequent weather changes and sometimes fierce storms. Fishers on the lake experienced lives fraught with suffering and peril. They often fished at night, when the wind and waves threatened to swamp their small, wooden, open boats. Furling the single sail and taking to the oars were the only means to escape wintry squalls, when the water was cold, icy in the wind, and their hands and faces grew numb. In milder weather, night fishing could be peaceful, if dull. Galilean fishers used hand-made nets spread wide over the water to catch their prey.

The Sea of Galilee was at the center of political and religious divisions. In the first few decades, *Anno Domini*, Decapolis bordered Gaulanitis, east of the Sea of Galilee, governed by Philip, son of Herod the Great. Herod Antipas, also a son of Herod the Great, ruled Perea as well as Galilee, west across the Lake; the region of Decapolis separated his two principalities. Northeast of Decapolis was rocky Trachonitis. Panias lay to the north, below Mount Hermon. Bordering Decapolis on the southwest was Samaria, the land between Galilee and Judaea, a hilly, fruitful land home to the Samaritans; north of Samaria was Phoenicia, the coastal land next to the Mediterranean of the ancient cities of Tyre and Sidon. The fertile lands about the Sea of Galilee hosted roads from the Mediterranean Sea to

Damascus in Syria, which were busy with trade and travelers. News and rumor spread quickly. The varied Jewish and Gentile cities surrounding the lake were populous and cosmopolitan.

The peoples of Judaea, Samaria, and Galilee worshiped the God of Abraham, while the peoples of Decapolis were polytheistic Greek Gentiles. They were heirs to a religious and cultural tradition that dated back several thousand years in which poets, playwrights, and philosophers tried to make sense of their world. The grip of fear enabled arrogant, violent people who tried to hide their fear through chaos and conquest to take control of the vast, silent, terrified majority. No one could equal the aggression, narcissism, and hubris of King Herod.

King Herod and his successors were not Jews, rather Idumeans who ruled Judaea at the pleasure of the Romans. Herod had in youth been a warlord fighting rival claimants to power in Judaea, Samaria, and Galilee among other Jewish, Idumean, Syrian, Arabian, and Roman warlords. In the wake of Alexander the Great's conquests, the various peoples of Palestine and surrounding regions had experienced Greek kings fighting against local peoples and among themselves for control. The ruling dynasty of Antigonids controlling the vast Seleucid Empire, which stretched from the eastern shores of the Mediterranean to Persia, were like most kings vain and jealous of power, unwilling to share the adoration of their subjects even with the divine, of which they came to believe they were a part.

Ancient writers, faced with fantastic characters of myth and legend who rivaled the gods, though they were mere mortals, counseled their readers against hubris. Ancient kings of the East —the Egyptians and the Persians for example—had constantly to be reminded that they were humans, not gods. Greek poets, playwrights, and philosophers described how hubris was the unmaking of many humans who elevated themselves above their station. It was to combat hubris and to arrive at a realistic assessment of humanity and its relation to the divine that many Greeks turned to philosophy.

Vanity and ambition often overwhelm philosophy, which was the case with the Greek kings of Asia. Hubris destroyed them all. An annoyance to their personal worship was the Hebrew worship of Yahweh, who would countenance no challengers to His power and glory. Kings such as Antiochus Epiphanes, literally "god made manifest," sought to eliminate the worship of Yahweh, substituting images of the Greek god Zeus even in the Temple of Jerusalem, the center of the worship of Yahweh. Antiochus' actions inspired rebellion by the Maccabeans, Jewish rebels who fought for national pride and for the sake of Yahweh. But even with the defeat of foreign kings, the Jews fell to squabbling among themselves, which provided an opening for any outside force with the strength in military might and stamina to conquer and not relinquish power.

The Romans had been inching into Asia since the beginning of the second century, *Ante Christos*, had pushed Antiochus III out of Greece, and had expanded their power into Anatolia. By the end of the second century, the Seleucid kings had been humbled by the Romans and a new power emerging in Asia, the Parthians. Rome and Parthia sought the region east of the Mediterranean and west of Persia as a buffer against the other. Roman generals in the first century, *Ante Christos*, took control of the peoples of Palestine. Gnaeus Pompey the Triumvir established his power in the region, appointing subordinate generals at the head of several legions of Roman soldiers to govern the region of Syria, Samaria, and Judaea. One of these governors, Gabinius, established an aristocratic rule at the pleasure of the Romans in Judaea.

Upon the ascension of Julius Caesar to total power in Rome,

Antipater, a warrior vying for power in Judaea, earned Caesar's favor, and became High Commissioner of Judaea, appointed by the Romans. Antipater was from the region of Idumaea, south of Judaea. Antipater's son Herod helped his father establish control throughout Palestine, then succeeded him. Herod learned the proper obsequiousness toward the Romans, and the first emperor Octavian Caesar, to keep his power for over thirty years. Herod was appointed King of Judaea by the Roman generals Octavian and Mark Antony He was an energetic ruler who sought to maintain his personal power at all costs. He supported Judaism and lavished money (gained through ruinous taxation of the people) on his own palaces, in the building of cities (such as Caesarea), and on Jerusalem. Like other Asian kings, Herod struggled with hubris, often confusing himself with the divine, rarely feeling the humility of humanity. He was succeeded upon his death by his son Herod Archelaus, who imitated his father in all his faults, insecurities, vanity, and willingness to be deceived.

The Herods ruled over their subjects in Galilee, Samaria, and Judaea with selfish brutality. Herod Archelaus, upon taking the throne, proceeded to massacre people in Jerusalem who called his legitimacy into question. Human rights did not exist, no matter if a king or a Roman general or procurator ruled. Individuals could be summarily arrested, tortured on the rack, and executed, dying the slow painful death of crucifixion. The people cowered in fear as individuals, only rarely testing their strength and courage as a brute mass of violent humanity. The Romans were only too good at ruthless annihilation of rebellion, and the people were repeatedly cowed by the strength of the sword.

The Romans of the first century ruled a society in which mysticism and credulity mixed with attempts at rational thought and skepticism, when fundamental assumptions, basic rules and accepted traditions, were sufficiently rigid to become antithetical to all supposition. Hypocrisy overwhelmed the wise as well as the ignorant, the leaders as well as the led. Mirroring changing time, it was a culture of diversity and movement, cosmopolitan yet traditional, overtly stagnant but within were swirling currents of conflict and uncertainty. Society and culture were deeply in need of something. The primitive and sophisticated stood side by side. Barbarism countered civilized behavior. At the same time as there were large cities, trade, and advances in science, architecture, and medicine, the society was marred by a love of violence, ongoing rivalries and conflicts, dependence on the natural environment, famine and disease, ignorance and uncertainty. Humans aggressively pursued wealth, power, honor, immortality, and knowledge only to come up short on all accounts. Human weakness, ignorance, frivolity, suffering, aggression, and sinfulness were never more apparent than during the time of the Herods.

King Herod, like so many monarchs and warriors of the past, suffered from physical and mental ailments. Deceived by evil and love of self, personal disaster plagued him. He was surrounded by flatterers and connivers, even among his family. Unable to trust anyone, he suspected everyone, and lived in fear. Dissent and conspiracy resulted in the execution of Herod's wife Mariamme, and three of his sons: Alexander, Aristobulus, and Antipater. Seemingly punished for the many great sins against his family, Herod died a slow, wasting death in which his bowels became ridden with intestinal worms.

Ancient philosophers and theologians believed that God, however manifested in a particular religion, would repay those who hurt others, who lived only for their own power and wealth, who put themselves above Himself. The first century writer

Plutarch, in *Why God is Slow to Punish*, argued from the perspective of Greek and Roman philosophy that punishment awaited those who transgressed the laws and God's ways. They may seem to flourish from their evil actions, but that is only because time blinds human perception. God acts in His time. Likewise, the Hebrews believed that Yahweh will punish— eventually. The Psalmist constantly predicted that those who do evil will suffer accordingly. Psalm 1 tells us that the impious "are like the dust that the wind flings from off the land." They "will not rise up in judgment, nor sinners in the council of the righteous, because the Lord knows the way of the righteous, and the way of the impious will perish."

Such knowledge, of the future sufferings of the sinful, did not lead to comfort among the pious. The Psalmist knew, for example, that his own actions would fall short notwithstanding his intentions. "Behold," he wrote in Psalm 51, "I was brought forth in iniquity, and in sin did my mother conceive me." Human happiness was after all never the lot of humankind, as the many Greek poets, tragedians, and historians taught. Greek myths pictured the fates determining the lot of humankind and the furies pursuing those who attempted to rise above, or alter, their fate. Such were the themes of the Greek tragic playwrights Aeschylus, Sophocles, and Euripides.

Indeed, the point of religion and philosophy, as the Apostle Paul argued, is to remind humans of their shortcomings and to raise the bar of achievement to such an impossible height that failure, hence misery, is the only possible result.

3

THE TERROR OF NATURE AND THE DIVINE

There is a moment in *Prometheus Bound*, the tragedy by the Greek playwright Aeschylus, where Prometheus, having been chained to a lonely crag in the Caucasus Mountains by Hephaistos on orders of Zeus, king of gods, declares to his hearers, the Daughters of Oceanus, that "I stopped mortals from seeing their fate in advance.... I settled unseeing hopes to dwell among them." This was a strange gift from the benefactor of humankind. Prometheus was unable to teach foresight to humans, so he gave them the dubious gift of the ability to ignore their common fate. To these doomed creatures who happily ignore their doom, he also gave the arts and sciences that comprise human civilization. Prometheus, whose name means foresight, knew all along his terrible fate, and he knew as well of his eventual release. He was aware of Zeus's plan to destroy humankind: brutish, primitive creatures little better than animals. As Hesiod explains, Zeus refused to allow humans the gift of fire, which would change them for the better; Prometheus stole the fire, hiding a spark in a fennel-stalk. Humans, with the gift of fire, changed their ways and rose above other creatures. Prometheus tells the Daughters of Oceanus, in Aeschylus's version of the myth, that he found humans "helpless at first, and made them able to reflect and use their wits." They were aimless, blind creatures who "acted in every matter without intelligence, till I revealed to them the risings of the stars and settings hard to judge. And then I found for them the art of using numbers, that master science, and arrangement of letters, and a discursive memory." He taught humans how to use chariots, how to sail the seas, "soothing medicines," and the "ways of prophecy." In short, "Prometheus gave all arts and sciences to men."[1]

Thousands of years later, human civilization continues to be molded along the lines that Aeschylus metaphorically described. Humans have developed from Prometheus' gift of fire a technological control over the environment to ensure a comfortable existence. Humans have learned quickly the arts to develop a variety of modes of expression, countless media to record, communicate, and create. Knowledge of medicine and the sciences have unlocked secrets of the human body, the earth, and the heavens. But for all this, humans remain "creatures of a day," unable to acquire Prometheus' talent of foresight, granted only the ability to forget that we are "impotent, . . . weak as a dream," doomed to live our existence in blind confusion, uncertain of the future.[2] Granted the power to shape material existence, nevertheless humans lack the knowledge commensurate with such power. Armed with technology yet uncertain of the future, humans have historically lashed out in a blind attempt to extend power over something, anything. Control becomes the panacea for ignorance of the future. Living moment by moment, insecure in existence, lacking Promethean foresight, control is the means by which humans face the legion of fear.

The moment when the transition occurred from *Ante Christos* to *Anno Domini* was like all moments: people were completely dependent upon the past yet in utter expectation of the future. Contemplation of the past brought disillusion to those who could see the bleak and dark colors of suffering, pain, ignorance, hunger, poverty, disease, violence, and war. The faint possibility that the future might bring a change, some fulfillment to the past, to end the consequences of sin, gave people hope. But it was hope compressed within the narrow confines of the present, of time, therefore of the institutions, society, assumptions, and expectations of the passing moment. Disaster and disappointment had hitherto comprised the story of human existence, the pattern of civilization throughout the ages. Falsehood, deception, sin, and evil confronted those who sought in the past, present, and future truth and goodness. Sermons and writings of priests and prophets praising the divine on the vast wonder of Creation, on the goodness and mercy of providence, seemed but hollow words to people who experienced the dismal consequences of sin, the apparent wrath of Heaven. Benefactors of humankind came to horrible ends and everlasting torment at the hands of the very gods to which humans prayed for help and redemption.

Prometheus, one such benefactor, was tormented every day in the Caucasus mountains by a vulture that tore at his liver—a hedonistic organ that stimulates in humans the desire for more—which would regenerate at night so to provide the same torturous meal the next day.

The notion that the divine is found in mountain regions is very ancient. Highlands are forbidding, elusive, distant home of the divine, blazing in the sunlight one minute, hidden from sight another. Storm clouds steal upon the high peaks, mesmerizing, stifling. Bone-chilling cold startles the ill-prepared traveler, who prays for the sun, which comes soon enough, and with it the wind, razor-sharp, searing, eroding all but the hardiest forms of life that retreat to the cracks and crevices of the rocky summits. Life hangs on amid chaos, as did Prometheus.

Mountain sides host a spectacle of descending waters, from drips and trickles of the coolest, clearest dew to the sum of waters, the raging torrent that tosses all things about in its path, a cascade the force and destiny of which is determined from above, rushing from the past to the future, and the sea. Moisture seeks the quickest descent, and rivers gather the waters of highlands to rush into valleys, destroying all in its wake. Ancient myths retain the memory of massive floods in the distant past, which destroyed and killed and terrorized.

The most ancient of the accounts of a vast deluge that implanted itself upon the human mind, never to be forgotten, is found in the *Epic of Gilgamesh.* This story derives from mythological events during the third millennium, *Ante Christos*, when there had developed a sophisticated human society in Mesopotamia, ancient Iraq. Here, such city-states as Ur, Eridu, Kish, Lagash, and Nippur in the Tigris and Euphrates river valleys boasted tens of thousands of inhabitants. Thick walls and ramparts surrounded these busy metropolises, which featured extensive trade, the production of crafts, specialization of labor, a multi-layered social structure, and monumental architecture. The government was as organized as the economy; priests served as conduits for divine instructions from patron deities; scribes recorded the decisions of gods and men. Writing, created to account for surplus wealth and trade, developed into an expression of human hopes, fears, and aspirations. Once humans had reached the capacity to guarantee a surplus of food year after year, to gain greater control over existence and to ensure survival beyond the moment, they were free to speculate on the future and to recall the past—a *human* future and past that was not quite the same as the natural (or divine) future and past. Humans—separate, distinct, unique—began to try to explain their origins, past and possible future, in human terms.

The *Epic of Gilgamesh* reveals the awareness of what is human, detached from nature, and a sense of confidence that explanations exist for the mysteries of the universe, which dominate human existence. Ancient Mesopotamian literature not only conceptualizes the forces of nature with a set identifiable pantheon of gods and goddesses, but also elevates the stature of humans to semi-divine status; hence the hero Gilgamesh was part divine, part human, though fully mortal respecting death. The gods themselves had human traits, which shows that ancient Mesopotamians were sufficiently confident to bring nature and the divine down to a human level (since the reverse was impossible). Gilgamesh traveled to the ends of the earth seeking the secret of eternal life; but he failed. The *Epic of Gilgamesh* features the story of an ancient deluge, in which a heroic ark-builder, Utnapishtim, gathered his family and pairs of animals into a boat to ride out the great flood. For this the gods granted Utnapishtim eternal life. Gilgamesh went in search of this god-man, only to discover that humans cannot escape death, their common fate.

Death is the only event about which a human can be sure. Everything else about the future is unclear. For the ancient Mesopotamians, an anonymous, mysterious fate spun the course of the fabric of each human life. Each human had a destiny; but what was it? All that Gilgamesh and the people of his time could gleam from life and nature were vague, sporadic hints, provided by the gods or inherent in the order of things, that tantalized one with indications of *what might be*. Fate bound the gods themselves, who had more knowledge than humans about the course of things, but just as little power to alter them. Humans might cajole or persuade the gods to act on their behalf in various matters; but once an event was fated, nothing could change it. Not surprisingly, then, the Mesopotamians and other peoples of the ancient Near East looked at the universe, which operated according to an inherent inner law of nature, with astonishment, fear, and piety. They were as children before a divine parent, helpless, dependent, begging for consideration, passively awaiting *what will be*. But this parent was deaf to the appeals of the child; this parent was unseen, unheard, invisible except for the residue of its actions, the stuff of human history.

The fear of the unknown experienced by ancient humans was recorded over and again in verse and narrative. The peoples of the second millennium, *Ante Christos*, in and about the Mediterranean basin waged a war of fear against the depths of the sea. The mariners of ancient Phoenicia, Crete, and Greece, particularly the voyagers of the Aegean and Ionian seas, used the sea as a route for trade and conquest. Ocean depths spawned fears of tempests and monsters, castaways and a watery death, that were expressed by poets and historians in later years.

The patterns of wind and sea mirror primordial human feelings. There is constancy and continuity in the rolling waves and unsurpassed sameness of the ocean. The deep wine blue mystery hides unfathomable life and "reflects the face of heaven."[3] The sharp salt breeze refreshes and pinches thoughts from the mind. Yet intermittent shoals break the sameness of the sea. They are elusive, hidden, scarcely revealing themselves in the spray that rises from conflict. Elsewhere craggy rocks rise and fall to the heartbeat of the waves. Water surges in and out, hiding then revealing the sandy shore that momentarily, again and again, waits in peace. Meanwhile, distant clouds floating on the horizon lull one to passivity. Hence does the emptiness of the mind mirror the emptiness of the sea. Into such barrenness time brings the distant gray sky to bear. Soon the torrent engulfs all in its path, bringing the terror of change and movement. Then once again calm. The humid world of the sea casts fog all about, which envelops, hides, the path of the storm's destruction

Ancient peoples personalized, anthropomorphized, the vastness of the depths of the sea, the terror of the unknown beneath the surface, the unrelenting storms that give no quarter, into supernatural beings: Pontus the sea; Nereus the old man of the sea; Nereids the sea nymphs; Thalassa the old woman of the sea; Oceanus the world encircling ocean; Oceanids, sea nymphs; Proteus the deity of the changes in the sea; Poseidon the Olympian god of the sea; Amphitrite wife of Poseidon; Triton the messenger of the sea; and a variety of monsters: gorgons, harpies, sirens. Homer relates that Odysseus experienced the call of the sirens, the call of the depths of the sea, the beckoning toward death that mariners experience, as well as horrible monsters, the nightmarish Scylla and Charybdis. And Odysseus was not alone. Homer's *Odyssey* provides a beautiful account of the legion of fear that gripped the lives of ancient mariners.

Nature, represented by the gods, particularly at sea, could hardly be predicted, was whimsical like an indecisive child, angry then calm, violent then passive, one minute the sea a glassy mirror, the next the churning waves threatening to swamp and destroy anything, anyone, in its path. Homer, whoever he was, whether a blind poet or a host of poets, a person who had experienced action in war and on the sea or someone having heard warriors and mariners give so many tales that it formed an accurate lore of the conflict of human with nature, expressed the terror of the Greeks, the Achaeans, when faced with the power and mysterious depths of the wine-dark sea. Menelaus told Telemachus of his adventurous voyage home from Troy, being driven away from the Aegean coast toward Egypt, where he found refuge then felt marooned on the island of Pharos. Only when he could cajole the secrets of the deep from the beings that dwelt therein—Nereids and Nereus—was he able to discover the means to leave the island prison. Homer says that the Achaeans had to capture Nereus and hold him, as he changed shape from one terrible image to another, from one moment to another, before the god would reveal the future and what it held for Menelaus, his family, and companions.

Likewise Odysseus, stranded on the island of Calypso in the Western (Mediterranean) Sea, could not fathom an escape across this sea east back home to Greece, telling Calypso, after she suggested that he build a boat to sail away, that even the most sea-worthy ships could scarcely cross that wild and terrifying sea. After she convinced him, however, and he set sail, he confronted the true character of the Mediterranean, personified by Poseidon, who sent crashing waves driven by hurricane winds in all directions and torrential rain, which swamped his boat and almost drowned Odysseus. The story of his days on the sea, holding on to a piece of wood from the destroyed boat, his arrival to the land of the Phaiakians, his undaunting urge to live, finding escape from the surging surf crashing into rocks, his arrival in a peaceful river, crawling ashore, finding a nest of leaves to bury himself in for protection, is an elegant tale of human survival of all of life's fears.

At least the Phaiakians represented a semblance of an orderly society, unlike the islands in which the goddess Calypso and the witch Circe wielded arbitrary power over nature and humans. Other islands on the vast sea were desolate and savage, as Odysseus experienced on the island of the Cyklops. Here, the foolishly courageous Achaeans faced the brutal aggression of a monster, a giant who knew nothing of custom and hospitality, the means by which humans tried to order their existence. The Achaeans experienced some of the greatest fears known to humans: being trapped, without escape; being subject to the whims of a killer who treats the human as an animal and source of food; experiencing wanton murder and consumption of human flesh while others look on in horror; experiencing closely the randomness of life and death.

Homer anthropomorphized all aspects of nature, such as the winds, making them subject to the power of Aelius; the forest, inhabited, personalized by nymphs and such nature deities; human emotions, such as love, hate, foreboding, jealousy; human savagery, represented by those humans transformed into animals by the witch Circe. Homer's story tells us how humans, being tempted and beguiled by pleasure and softness, can become uncivilized brutes. Faced with the animal part of us, it terrifies, the savagery within. The first century essayist Plutarch, in his whimsical take on the episode, discussing the purported irrationality of animals, argued that the savage animal within humans allows for contentment, whereas the human promethean character means discontent.

The utter unknown of death was likewise anthropomorphized by Homer. Odysseus in the land of the dead faced his own death conversing with the shades of those he once knew—Achilles, Agamemnon, his mother—the terrifying gloom of the future, of the passing from life to a dreary existence of no return, and worse, the passing of friends and loved ones whom we recall merely by the shadows of their memory. Death, the future: there are so many ways it could come to Odysseus, to all humans. It is the one certainty, the one event known of the future, and yet it is unknown: the time, the place, the occasion. The secret of death is the secret of the unknown. Odysseus characteristically faced this unknown mystery as anthropomorphized by the sirens, monstrous beings who by their beautiful, unearthly voices call humans to what can be, the potential for pleasure and happiness, but who bring doom to the willing listener. Odysseus listened to their song of the uncertain future and the consequent fear that such uncertainty brings—it is a call of the wild, the call of the primitive, the call of disorder, ultimate freedom, anarchy, chaos, danger; the call of the past, of what could have been; call of the future, of what could be. The call destroys those crazed by time, temptation, savagery, loss of self. Odysseus by tying himself to the ship's mast hears the call, the present terror, the edge between past and future. By experiencing the present, he faces the fears of the present and it drives him temporarily insane, but with it comes knowledge and awareness.

Legion's self-imposed exile among the tombs of the dead was itself an odyssey of the experience of danger and foreboding and the crazed response of the fearful man, who is uncertain where to turn, which path to take, what the future holds, what direction the past suggests.

Legion wondered, as did countless others: Is this life, filled with pathos and suffering, all there is? Humans throughout the ancient world at the end of the first millennium, *Ante Christos*, sought a promise of something more, life beyond life. Cults devoted to deities such as Dionysus (Bacchus, god of the vine), Demeter (goddess of grain), Isis (Egyptian fertility goddess), Asclepius (god of healing), Orpheus (the musician), and Cybele (Anatolian mother goddess), became exclusive to those worshipers who practiced their secret rites. Initiation into the mysteries of the faith included purification by fasting, washing, even corporeal punishment; a sacred meal and drink; and an emotional experience of union with the god.

The mysteries were solemn, yet often highly emotional. The assumption of a mind/body duality, that the body must be suppressed so that the mind or soul can be released, united the mystery cults with more formal philosophies. Mystery cults typically had a savior or a god once a man, sometimes born of a virgin, son of the ultimate reality or God, who would live and die then experience resurrection—the ideal man resurrected to a divine status. The mystic devotee to the worship of Asclepius, who lived a century after Legion, Aelius Aristides, experienced communion, almost friendship, with the god in dreams, hearing from the god that "thou art uniquely chosen" to serve him.[4] At one point Aristides "thought I touched the God and felt him near, I myself at the time being in a condition between waking and sleeping."[5] Indeed, the goal of the mysteries was union, or identification, with god—to be like or be god. Initiation rites brought out the god from within the mind or soul into a mystical union.

It is doubtful that Legion of Decapolis had such a profound experience, though sometimes mystics, because of their sensitivity, their intuition, their empathy, can feel much fear. Perhaps he was attracted to the mysteries of Ascelpius, the healing god, whose worshipers slept at night in the god's temple hoping for a dream to direct them upon awakening toward the path of healing. Legion, who sought healing for his ailment, listened intently to travelers when they spoke of places they had been, and healers they had witnessed.

At the same time, the Hellenistic world in which Legion lived had a long tradition lasting hundreds of years of skeptical thinkers who were constantly seeking, questioning, resisting. As Legion matured into a thinking, reflective individual he was most attracted to those who asked the same questions he asked, who were as confused by life as he was, who had their own legion of memories and guilt, who also struggled with the Fear.

Many professed to *know*: Sophists, Academics, Peripatetics, Epicureans, Stoics, Cynics, Skeptics. Notwithstanding the grand ideas of Platonic and Aristotelian reasoning, Cartesian mechanics and the scientific method, the discoveries in physics and chemistry during the past century, life is pretty much the same no matter the place or time: a daily grind of work to survive, daily prayers to whatever unseen force might help with perplexing problems, daily struggles with pain and fear and illness. Poverty, depression, hunger, disease, apathy, malaise—such continues the way of humankind.

The greatest human accomplishments have come about in response to fear. Thales, Protagoras, Anaxagoras, Xenophanes, Socrates, and other Greek thinkers sought to explain the universe by imposing the structure of the human mind upon it, to conceptualize it so to understand it. They broke from the primitive anthropomorphism of their forebears to create a universe that resembled the human mind, that was created by, dominated by, mind (*nous*) itself.

Yet, as the prophet in the *Odyssey* wisely said (as translated by Robert Fitgerald): "Of mortal creatures, all that breathe and move, earth bears none frailer than mankind. What man believes in woe to come, so long as valor and tough knees are supplied him by the gods? But when the gods in bliss bring miseries on, then willy-nilly, blindly, he endures. Our minds are as the days are, dark or bright, blown over by the father of gods and men."[6]

This, then, was the human quandary, as elucidated by the myth of Prometheus, the *Epic of Gilgamesh,* and the poems of Homer: how can humans, who perceive the future, who know the doom that awaits, who therefore live each moment in fear of the next, face this fear, confront it with action, use the superior human mind to grab hold of the future and make it conform to a human image, and by molding the future, conquer fear?

Greek philosophers long believed that philosophy, science, and mathematics, understanding natural phenomena, were the means to the end of human control. The Pre-Socratic Greek scientists of the seventh, sixth, and fifth centuries spawned scientific inquiry throughout the Mediterranean world, especially at Athens in the fifth and fourth centuries. The student of Socrates, Plato, and his student Aristotle, developed sophisticated theories of the nature of reality, cause and effect, and explanations of natural and human phenomena. Such philosophers constantly sought, questioned, resisted. They were confused by life, had their own Legion of memories and guilt, struggled with Fear. Indeed, ancient writers—Homer, Herodotus, Plutarch, Livy, Caesar, Suetonius, Tacitus, Thucydides, Arrian, Xenophon, Virgil, Polybius, Hesiod, Catullus, Dio Cassius, Ammianus Marcellinus, Seneca, Lucretius, Julian, Libanius, Sophocles, Aristophanes, Euripides, Aeschylus, Juvenal, Sallust, Pliny, and Marcus Aurelius—seem most familiar with the stuff of fear. Philo Judeaus believed that philosophers are healers of souls, "which are under the mastery of terrible and almost incurable diseases, which pleasures and appetites, fears and griefs, and covetousness, and follies, and injustice, and all the rest of the innumerable multitude of other passions and vices, have inflicted upon them." Perhaps. But even so great a philosopher as Marcus Aurelius believed that failure and fear defined his life and times during the Pax Romana. In *Meditations*, he lamented, "in the life of a man, his time is but a moment, his being an incessant flux, his senses a dim rushlight, his body a prey of worms, his soul an unquiet eddy, his fortune dark, and his fame doubtful." The poet of the *Epic of Gilgamesh*, the poet of

Ecclesiastes, lamented the brief time and insignificance that humans experience on Earth. Fear and anxiety compelled Boethius to declare: "hastened by unhappiness has age come upon me without warning, and grief hath set within me the old age of her gloom." Such has been the theme of other reflective thinkers throughout the ages.[7]

All lives contain the sources of discontent. In each age, such as antiquity, there exists a legacy of a violent past: of the Trojan War, the Peloponnesian War, the Roman civil wars, the Maccabean War, the Jewish War. Likewise, in each life there exists a legacy of trials and grief. The perceptive observer is often haunted by the manifold human crimes that comprise the past. Thinkers are prey to the despair and depression that ruminators feel. Time disregards wisdom and grand thoughts in the inexorable movement toward dissolution.

The malevolence in the world, collectively among humans, and the malevolence within each human, apparent in ancient philosophy and religion, led many thinkers to question the human propensity to know. Aeschylus used the image of Prometheus as an apparent benefactor of humankind: someone who *knew*, and passed his knowledge along. A primeval titan with human characteristics, Prometheus defied the eternal mind and power, characterized by the god Zeus, saving humans from weakness before nature, even extinction. The acquisition of knowledge, humans embracing a promethean mindset, knowing their power to manipulate the world, resulted in sorrow rather than contentment. Prometheus inadvertently cursed humanity: aware of their distinction from the rest of creation, humans try to control the creation, but lack the commensurate foresight and awareness. Transient beings, humans give themselves the air of the transcendent. But it is folly.

Legion knew this folly. The curse of Prometheus is the

helpless feeling of incarceration. The soul cries out for freedom, and nothing seems more wonderful than to be a bird in flight, soaring high above, or a stallion fleet of foot, or just the air, blowing aimlessly yet freely. The sorrow of a destiny unfulfilled, incarcerated with the body, the future a blank slate of vanishing dreams. Time ends, chained to the present. The now becomes the always: never a change, never the new, never freedom.

4

AN AGE OF DECEPTION

The ancient world was filled with darkness, as the light of truth rarely entered into the minds, activities, and habits of the people. Deception in all its forms reigned. Humans ran from time and truth, living in the moment, seeking through physical pleasure, materialism, self-satisfaction, intoxication, the means to enjoy life before it was gone. If this life is all there is then the transcendent, that is, any kind of truth, does not exist. Without a sense of truth, to have only a truth in every moment, means that experiences that have the highest value, or rush, in the moment have meaning—such as the orgasm, the intoxicated high, the emotional rush from violence—any sensual experience that is immediate and not long lasting. And these momentary experiences, done to enjoy life in the instant, actually result in deadening the person to the meaningful truths of life. Love is universal, the most powerful transcendent truth, such that it requires exceptional deception to convince a person that something else is more important. Only the most powerful temptation, the most powerful and exhilarating momentary experience, can do this. The more powerful the more deceptive.

Hence, the world has tottered along over the centuries from war to war, disaster to disaster, plague to plague, crisis to crisis. Every day a new problem, a new disaster, a new concern, whether it be a madman attempting to conquer other peoples, or an outbreak of disease sweeping through villages, or a typhoon destroying all in its path. When in each moment a new cause of fear appears, it is natural to run and hide, to cover oneself with the blankets of stimulants, depressants, sex, fantasy, violence, money, power, and other such delusions.

In Legion's time of the first century, *Anno Domini*, humans had developed a host of techniques to respond to fear and its sources. Humans sought the means to exert control over the supernatural. Extending the individual self, but collectively, into the *Other* of which they are a part, ancient humans over the course of countless millenniums used magic, prophecy, and astrology to exercise influence, to exert a feeble control, over that which dwarfed them. In the process humans began to convince themselves that they ultimately can and will control the environment, other creatures, other humans, other powers, other thoughts, other beings.

Magic is the means by which a person with professed or actual skills seeks to sense and use the powers inherent in nature. The ancient world featured a large cast of magicians of varying names and skills: augurers, soothsayers, diviners, shamans, Chaldeans, magi, priests, prophets, astrologers. These people convinced themselves and others that they could determine fate and destiny, the purposes and will of the gods, and the future, based on natural phenomena: the flight of birds, the shape of a liver, celestial objects at night, astronomical incidents such as eclipses, fantasies and dreams. People, the low as well as the great, acted according to the predictions of magicians.

Chaldean sorcerers, those who followed Zoroaster, as well as the Gymnosophists of India, had a broad reputation throughout the Mediterranean world and beyond for magic, sorcery, and dream interpretation. The ever-credulous Roman scientist Pliny the Elder derided Chaldeans as typically false prophets, though he did not doubt their expertise in magic. The Roman commentator and biographer Diogenes Laertius identified Zoroaster as the founder of the magical arts of the Chaldeans. Hence their name, *magi*, those who use magic—the understanding of the hidden truths of the natural world—to gauge the future, however imprecisely.

Magic and sorcery were considered appropriate responses by which to resist fear. How does a person resist the countless images from the past of error, sin, wretchedness, lust, violence? How is a random thought, a sensation, an image, a horrible feeling in the pit of the stomach, the stark loneliness, the seclusion from reality, the temptation, the deception, the demonization of the mind, the overwhelming presence of *Legion* —how is it to be resisted?

If the origin of the fear can be controlled, then the fear itself, it stands to reason, can be controlled as well. If a person fears hunger and famine, and incantations and spells guarantee a successful hunt, then the origin of the fear is controlled by a set course of action. If Apollo Smintheus (the Rat God) brings plague to men by means of his arrows, as in the *Iliad*, the right prayers and sacrifices according to the direction of the soothsayer and prophet might stem the god's anger, halt the plague. Prophets predicting the future based on the hints of the past set the path to be followed. The sibyls of ancient Greece and Rome, oracles of the divine, informed the fearful of what might be. People of the past and present have continued to consult such oracles.

Even Greeks who were critical thinkers believed in the consultation of oracles. Plutarch wrote that the Platonists and Stoics believed divination involved intuitive insights into the divine. Often these insights are found in dreams; they hint of ways to manipulate the nature of the present and future. Yet in dreams are often found the wrong path, sent by the gods who deceive — deceitful, malevolent Hermes (Roman Mercury) often sent dreams to people just to confuse and horrify them. Fear deprives the person of sleep at night at the one time in existence when peace can be found, and quietude during the day because of recollection of the specters of the night. Even more, a person who fears the malevolent and capricious divine will not enjoy respite in death, rather continual haunting punishments. Not only the Greeks and Romans conjured up gods of terror such as Hades and vengeful spirits such as the Furies, but other cultures throughout the world conceived of similar supernatural beings. And the fearful rejected, in Plutarch's words, their "benignity for terror, their paternal affection for tyranny, their providence for cruelty, and their frank simplicity for savageness and brutality."[1]

Contemporaries of Legion knew of a culture to the east, across the Tigris and Euphrates rivers, that had in previous centuries struggled with the concept of the apparent presence of evil in existence. The well-traveled fifth-century *Ante Christos* historian Herodotus learned that the Zoroastrians were not anthropomorphic, that they refused to identify a polytheistic pantheon of deities. Rather, under the influence of a semi-mythical figure, Zoroaster, they conceived of a singular goodness, Mazda, or Ahuramazda, whose power was opposed by a singular malevolence, Ahriman.

Zoroastrianism is significant to the world in that it introduced a hitherto unknown concept to world religion that has ever since characterized many such religions. This is the concept of dualism, that there is good and evil in the world. The Good, Ahuramazda in the case of Zoroastrianism, was countered by the evil Ahriman. At least during some periods in the history of Zoroastrianism, Ahriman was considered a force of evil that was the equal to Ahuramazda. Generally, Zoroastrians believed that notwithstanding the tremendous power and influence of Ahriman, Ahuramazda was still ultimately the supreme force in the world and universe. This notion of a divine personification of evil went beyond the polytheistic belief in demons and evil spirits. Ahriman was an unrelenting force in constant contrast with Good. If the universe has such a dualistic quality of good and evil, Zoroastrians reasoned, then humans must as well. Indeed, the propensity of humans to commit sin, to do evil, was conveniently explained by the presence of an evil force or being that could inhabit one's body and mind, tempting and leading one into sin.

The concept of dualism in Zoroastrianism had an uncertain impact on subsequent religious beliefs. During Legion's time, Roman soldiers and travelers had brought to the empire a cult derived from Zoroastrianism, the worship of the savior god Mithras. According to Plutarch, Mithras was the mediator between light and darkness, between Ahuramazda and Ahriman, between the spirit and the body. Another derivative of Zoroastrianism was Manicheism, a religion based on the teachings of a third-century, *Anno Domini*, eastern mystic named Mani, who adopted the dualism of good and evil from Zoroastrianism. Manicheism taught that good and evil are material forces that inhabit the Earth, and the human body. Each human has a share of good and a share of evil. Dietary habits and style of living (eschewing meat, wine, sex) could guarantee more good than evil in one's body. The impact of Zoroastrian dualism on other religions is more uncertain, however. The idea of an evil force in the world in Judaism does not appear until the end of the first millennium, *Ante Christos*. The Hebrew adversary (Satan) is a vague figure in the Old Testament, often pictured as working with God rather than against him (in the *Book of Job*, for example). The development in Jewish (and Christian) thought of a true force of evil, the devil (Greek *diabolos*) does not appear until the writings of the New Testament, where this presence of evil is variously called Satan, the Devil, the Adversary, the Tempter, and the Evil One. New Testament writings imply that notwithstanding the presence and power of evil in the world, God always remains in control—hence Judeo-Christian belief does not have a straightforward dualism.

During Legion's time people considered demons to be the agents of Satan. Demons were supernatural beings whose power was subject to God's will—just like humans. Demons found an affinity with humans by being able to enter the conscious/subconscious minds of humans and "possess" them. Humans could be released from demonic possession by the power of God. According to the *Book of Revelation*, however, notwithstanding the ultimate power of God, such demons will continue to act in human affairs even after Christ's death, to the apparent end of time.

That thinkers and believers could conceive of Evil confronting Good derives from the human experience of continually fighting against the divine supernatural presence of goodness. The *Iliad*, for example, portrays the human struggle against destiny—a fight with the gods themselves. The huge plain of battle outside of the gates of Troy in which the heroes Achilles, Hector, Diomedes, and Odysseus fight is similar to the vast surface of the sea that Odysseus struggles against on his journey back to Ithaca. In both stories, Fear hides just below the surface, like a shark with its dorsal fin protruding just above the water; the whole of the dangerous animal, the mighty destructive teeth spelling doom, lies silent, barely below the surface, waiting to strike. In the *Iliad*, the Achaeans struggle against Aphrodite and Ares, who appear on the field of battle with the Trojans; in the *Odyssey*, Odysseus fights against Poseidon, whose hatred for the man results in multiple shipwrecks and the deaths of his companions. Homer's poems are metaphors for the human struggle to endure, to survive, to gain immortality. Hence do humans wage a war against truth, against what is real, against the divine.

Humans throughout time embrace idols, figments of the imagination that take away from the constant, transcendent truth to a momentary truth, a falsehood, a temporary fix, a fantasy that distracts from reality. Fantasy is an illusion of the moment, an illusion of the senses and desire, providing quick and easy, illusory, pleasure and satisfaction, but vanishing just as quickly, leaving doubt and dissatisfaction in its wake. Fantasy can never be long term because it is a mere bubble waiting to pop. The myriad bubbles of the imagination, of a fantasy world, crowd upon a human, blinding the human to what is real.

Legion was constantly tempted by these short-lived yet prolific bubbles, sent by the deceiver. Legion himself became a deceiver—and learned to doubt and deny the truth, to think only of the present fear, the terror in each moment of what might be about to happen. Legion became a deceiver of self, kidnapping his mind and body, imprisoning his sense of normality, his sense of rightness and goodness.

II
THE TRANSCENDENT

There came a moment when the supernatural intervened, and the presence of God was felt, a metamorphosis occurred, and fear was transfigured into love.

5

A VISION OF THE NIGHT

And the angel came in unto her...
The rules of time vanish in the world of dreams. The ruminating mind grazes, feasts, in the field of dreams, of images formed in the past, masking reality. And the path appears uncertain, the way seems unclear, the abyss appears nearby, as time terrorizes and fear is in a rapture of expectant images. Days pass, journeys end, resolutions come to the anguished heart, fears begin in the troubled mind, in just a few hours or minutes of sleep. Possibilities, fantastic and real, occur in dreams, and they seem true, reality itself, until someone stirs or a mockingbird calls to the state of wakefulness. When is a person awake when dream has such power, when fantasy and imagination strays upon, stays upon, the mind in an instant, in every conceivable moment?

Are dreams the wanderings of a fertile imagination, the fantastic ruminations of an unsettled spirit? Or, are dreams messages brought by restlessness stirring in the deep recesses of the mind? Are dreams part of a collective memory, archetypal images brought to the present from some hidden place in the distant past? Or, are dreams the images and words of a supernatural messenger from a time and place of no beginning or end, no space, volume, or depth? If the images of a dream are so vivid, if the conversations are so easily recalled; if the sights and sounds are etched on the mind and memory, never to be forgotten; then how can the dream not be real, how can the message be ignored?

Peoples of two thousand years ago were believers in *oneiromancy*, dream analysis, because of the divine origins of dreams and the importance of determining the correct interpretation upon which to base actions. The gods spoke to the Greeks, according to Homer, in dreams, personified by the god Oneiros. Homer's *Iliad* portrays the father of the gods Zeus ordering Oneiros to the Greek camp to bring the divine message through dreams. In the *Odyssey* Homer has Penelope say, regarding dreams (as translated by Robert Fitzgerald): "many and many a dream is mere confusion, a cobweb of no consequence at all. Two gates for ghostly dreams there are: one gateway of honest horn, and one of ivory. Issuing by the ivory gate are dreams of glimmering illusion, fantasies, but those that come through solid polished horn may be borne out, if mortals only know them."

Dreams invite acceptance of a reality that is indeterminable in time, a truth that cannot be broken down by the ways of the objective thinker. Before the sophistication of modern society, the rise of human intelligence in pure and applied science, the conquest and control of the many environments in which humans dwell, humans were thinkers of a different sort. Ancients were so sure that ethereal messages were divine that kings sought out whoever could explain their dreams—soothsayers and prognosticators, experts who could read divine messages in the flights of birds, the arrangements of the stars, the shape of the liver of a sacrificial animal.

The Roman physician Galen followed his dreams as a means of improving his medicine. Another Roman physician, Gennadius, became convinced that the soul was immortal according to a dream. Plutarch thought that dreams indicated a humoral imbalance. "For absurd dreams and irregular and unusual fantasies show either abundance or thickness of humors, or else a disturbance of the spirits within. For the motions of the soul show that the body is nigh a distemper. For there are despondencies of mind and fears that are without reason or any apparent cause, which extinguish our hopes on a sudden. Some there are that are sharp and prone to anger, whom a little thing makes sad; and these cry and are in great trouble when ill vapors and fumes meet together."[1] Artemidorus wrote *Oneirocritica*, in which he engaged in extensive analysis of dreams to determine their meaning. Aelius Aristides, the priest of the Greek god of healing Asclepius, kept records (*Sacred Teachings*) of his dreams for many years, assuming that the god spoke directly to him, giving him advice on healing and other matters. Although Aristotle wrote about the widespread practice of dream interpretation in his *On Prophesying by Dreams*, in which he had a scientific approach, discouraging the belief that the gods spoke to humans through dreams, the mass of people at his time and for subsequent centuries disagreed, and professional dream interpreters were in high demand.

Plutarch's essays provide some of the most sophisticated ancient thinking about dreams. In *Of Superstition*, he wrote wisely: "Fear alone, being equally destitute of reason and audacity, renders our whole irrational part stupid, distracted, and unserviceable." Fear binds and distracts. Superstitious people in dreams feel like they are "in the place of the damned" where "certain prodigious forms and ghastly spectres . . . tortures the unhappy soul." "The frightful visionary hath ne'er a world at all, either in common with others or in private to himself; for neither can he use his reason when awake, nor be free from his fears when asleep; but he hath his reason always asleep, and his fears always awake; nor hath he either an hiding-place or refuge." Zeno, Plutarch wrote, "thought that everybody might gauge his progress in virtue by his dreams, if he saw himself in his dreams pleasing himself with nothing disgraceful, and neither doing nor wishing to do anything dreadful or unjust, but that, as in the clear depths of a calm and tranquil sea, his fancy and passions were plainly shown to be under the control of reason." "Those, then, that have such pleasant, clear, and painless dreams, and no frightful, or harsh, or malignant, or untoward apparition, may be said to have reflections of their progress in virtue; whereas agitation and panics and ignoble flights, and boyish delights, and lamentations in the case of sad and strange dreams, are like the waves that break on the coast, the soul not having yet got its proper composure, but being still in course of being moulded by opinions and laws, from which it escapes in dreams as far as possible, so that it is once again set free and open to the passions." Vice hangs on to a person especially at night, "for during such a one's sleep the body indeed gets rest, but the mind has terrors, and dreams, and perturbations, owing to superstition." In sleep, the fantasies of vice have full reign.[2]

Ancient literature is replete with examples of criminals haunted by dreams. Plutarch, in *Concerning such Whom God is Slow to Punish*, provided the example of Apollodorus, the tyrannical demagogue of Potideia who, according to Diodorus, "aimed at tyranny, and thought to render the conspiracy secure, invited a young lad, one of his friends, to a sacrifice, slew him as an offering to the gods, gave the conspirators his vitals to eat, and when he had mixed the blood with wine, bade them drink it." Plutarch wrote that "Apollodorus in a dream beheld himself flayed by the Scythians and then boiled, and that his heart, speaking to him out of the kettle, uttered these words, I am the cause thou sufferest all this. And another time, that he saw his daughters run about him, their bodies burning and all in a flame."[3] Plutarch explained, in *A Discourse to an Unlearned Prince*: "the mind is vexed and distracted by it, as a distempered brain is with troublesome dreams, insomuch that it hath not strength enough to execute what it desires."[4] And in *Why the Oracles Cease*: "for sometimes we are mightily troubled with many and confused visions in our dreams, and at other times there is a perfect calm, undisturbed by any such images or ideas." "Melancholy people . . . are much subject to dreams in the night, and their dreams sometimes prove true."[5]

Plutarch, living a century after Legion, had a sophisticated explanation for the impact of dreams. But he, along with other philosophers, were unclear precisely where they originated. The less thoughtful were much more clear. People throughout the ancient Mediterranean believed that the divine spoke to humans through dreams.

Such was the experience of the young woman, which brought images so vivid, a conversation so easily recalled, that the sights and sounds etched on the mind and memory were never to be forgotten. Whether she was asleep or awake is indeterminable as it was recorded later; the experience was so vivid in her sleep as to be unquestionably real or so dreamlike in her wakefulness as to not be doubted. When the event happened, day or night, winter or summer, month or year, is unknown, unimportant. It was an experience not bound by the normal rules of time. How long it lasted, and whether it was continuous in one or several series of moments, is irrelevant to the experience, to the overwhelming truth that the message contained, both for her and for others. People of her time and of the past had had similar experiences, as she well knew, from hearing stories told or listening to the scriptures being read. She had learned that messengers came and spoke to royalty and commoners alike. Many were the experts who could identify apparent divine messages. She had no need for such expertise. Her experience was sufficient to know it was a messenger, one who came from God.

Strangely, in recollecting the experience, she did not describe the messenger save for his name, Gabriel, which means *man of God*, or *strength in God*, which was precisely what the girl, Mary, would require to fulfill the requirements of the message. It was an ethereal messenger who spoke to Mary, a messenger without form, merely the spoken word or thoughts, powerful enough to bring about a change in the girl, to cause her body to shutter in the presence of God, to hear more carefully the words spoken, to know for certain what was said to her in her mind.[6]

She was no one in particular, merely a girl, a virgin, daughter of commoners, illiterate and ignorant as were most such people two thousand years ago. At the same time she was exceptional, unique, one favored by God, selected by Him for an important role, a service for all humankind. Her purpose in life, like all girls and women of her time, was to marry and bear children, if she was so fortunate; few women questioned such a role, it was what their mothers and grandmothers had done, and what their daughters and granddaughters would do. To have a mate and have a child was as natural as to sleep and eat, to live and die. And yet the dreamlike message she experienced, which told her that this was her destiny, which was neither exceptional nor out of the ordinary, was forcefully put, a message of an imminent occurrence, something that could not be delayed. She was a virgin. And yet, she was to have a child. Her dream turned out to bear a divine gift.[7]

Modern philosophy and science are uncomfortable with the presence of God in any venue, much less the womb. What should be considered the most inviolable place has been violated and penetrated time and again to destroy the most sacred of all things, life. Great thinkers, such as Sigmund Freud, who saw God as the figment of the collective imagination, the product of psychic yearning for completion and love, believe there is no true unity with the divine, in or outside of the womb. Other great thinkers, such as Karl Marx, believing that biological demands precede consciousness, that before awareness is hunger, subject humans to the overwhelming dominance of time and place. Yet, ironically, now and in the past humans have engaged in an unending search for the divine, the discovery of which, it is thought, will yield answers to the many perplexing questions confronting humankind. Great have been the number of philosophers who ask the questions all humans ask and propose answers fit for their time and place. Rather than finding humility in the elusive search for truth, thinkers wallow in the hubris of *knowing*. All the while humans face the abyss of ignorance.

Dreams invite acceptance of the unreal, something outside of oneself. Individuals in any culture at any time feel an overwhelming need for completion, sense a pull from a transcendent *other*. What Rudolph Otto called the *numinous* was the dazzling light that blinded Paul of Tarsus; the child's voice that responded to Aurelius Augustine's agonizing question; the austere, universal presence of the *One* that so captivated Plotinus and his disciples Porphyry and Julian; the oneness that Siddhartha Gautama experienced in the rushing water of the river of life; and the fear and awe that Moses knew when standing on holy ground before Yahweh. All of these religious experiences involve particular people at particular times seeking, sensing, reaching out for, receiving, and accepting, the transcendent.

The greatest threats to modern society in the third millennium, *Anno Domini*, are not overpopulation, hunger, disease, terrorism, global warming, and war—although these are pressing problems to be sure. Rather, the modern scientific worldview of purposeful objective thought is destroying the subjective, intuitive awareness of the numinous and transcendent that humans have sensed for countless ages. The individual's sense of self is a casualty in the secularization of knowledge that has occurred during the past two centuries. Impersonal social and economic forces rather than life are the great agents of change. Reason and science have overwhelmed intuition and art; the subject who intertwines oneself with the object of inquiry is condemned as biased and prejudiced; personal religious beliefs have no place in scholarly endeavors. This secular, objective trend is, perhaps, a mere aberration in time. The period from the structured urban lifestyle that began in Mesopotamia five thousand years ago to today is comparatively brief in the history of humankind. The age of modern science since 1500 is on the human time scale just a fleeting moment. The transcendent and the transient, the subjective and the objective, intuition and reason, have been united from the beginning of humankind.

Mary's betrothed similarly received a dreamlike visitor, a messenger bearing a gift, who asked of him to accept what he did not understand, to abide by a will larger than himself. Joseph, a simple man who worked with his hands, not a great thinker or exceptional leader, rather a person content to listen and abide, dreamed of God's messenger telling him to accept a destiny that would have otherwise been abhorrent to him. Betrothal to a virgin implied she would be untouched until marriage, that her womb was reserved for his seed. Joseph dreamed, however, that Mary was pregnant and that her womb was inviolable and sacred and that he must accept the child as his own. He awoke to a new reality that he acted upon with confidence in the truth. He transformed his entire life according to a message he received in a singular, inexact moment of time.

Joseph was a Hebrew, a Semite, a descendant of people who had migrated from ancient Iraq, Mesopotamia, west to the land of Canaan, what in time became Galilee, Samaria, and Judaea. The *Book of Genesis* describes the transformation of these Semites into Hebrews by focusing upon the story of a man, Abram, and his wife, Sarai, nomadic herders who followed a divine call to journey to a distant land. Like other Semites, Abraham and Sarah and their people continued to feel the terror of the unknown, but their fear was mitigated by the realization of a God who cared for them, who was Himself Fate, who controlled all things, and who could circumvent the laws of nature should He so desire. This identification of self with God grew more sophisticated with the passing centuries. We find in *Exodus* Moses discovering a God of law and deliverance called simply, "I Am Who I Am." Who precisely this God is and what are His powers and interest in humans is made specifically clear in the writings of the Psalmist David, king of the united kingdom of Israel and Judah from 1000 to 961, *Ante Christos*. David, at the same time a warrior, murderer, adulterer, and conqueror, was also a poet and singer of extraordinary talent and sensitivity, whose Psalms express the epitome of piety and anguish, love and torment.

David's poems are ironic expressions of faith in an all-powerful God even as evil torments and controls the poet. David discovered the dreamlike existence of continually being seduced by some force, some spirit, something strangely in yet outside himself. It was there to counter whatever felt good, those pleasant feelings of life, when things appear right, more than adequate, and nothing is better than a peaceful smile and soft sensations of contentment. It was a fleeting sensation, this intrusion into constancy and order, this violation of satisfaction and happy thoughts. It pierced well-being. It distracted normalcy. It penetrated into a deep well of abandonment, fear, distrust, envy, selfishness, anger, and lust. It found the weakness of his being, the entrance in time of corruption, the fleeting path to what is not real, the moment when fantasy, indolence, hunger, dissatisfaction, and the corporeal reign. It was not right yet it felt good. It was wrong yet just for a moment it was allowed. Evil triumphed. But only in the passing moments. God triumphed over the timeless, the transcendent feelings and experiences that overwhelmed the singular instance of evil.

God, Yahweh, transcends the moment by speaking in a timeless fashion. Sometimes his words are profound, as to Moses. Usually they are indirect, as to Elijah, when he heard God whispering to him. Sometimes the voice of God is found in the wind. The Hebrews discovered that God often speaks subtly, as through dreams. Elihu, in the *Book of Job*, proclaimed that God's word comes to humans "in a vision of the night," and He tells them of His plans, and dissuades them from their's.

Many Hebrew prophets were experts in dream interpretation. Joseph the son of Jacob became the powerful adviser to pharaoh after providing an insightful interpretation of the Egyptian ruler's dream. After failing to find his own dream prophesiers able to explain his perplexing dreams, the Babylonian king Nebuchadnezzar employed Daniel, who provided the correct interpretation. The Hebrew prophets heard the voice of God in singular and transcendent moments, either when awake or asleep, and responded like Isaiah, who declared, "the Spirit of the Lord God is upon me."

Isaiah, learning of God's plans, even predicted that at some point in time, "Behold, a virgin shall conceive, and bear a son, and shall call his name Immanuel." God is with us.

6

ASTRAL BECKONING

Behold, there came wise men from the east to Jerusalem . . . The world was in need of a savior; then a star appeared, an astral phenomenon seen in the east.

Those who witnessed the rising star on the endless desert horizon were seeking signs of the will of heaven, the becoming—that which is not, yet will be. Each night these sorcerers of the desert, star worshipers known as Chaldeans or magi (μάγος, magŏs), sought in the movement of the stars and planets along the zodiac the signs of the future, information they could employ in their sorcery and charms, their advice to kings, their own achievement of power and wealth. The astral event, unexpected, astonishing, and concerning, impelled the sorcerers to journey in search of its meaning.

Their search led them to the one through whom all of the past as well as the whole of the present and the future are fulfilled.

The sorcerers lived in lands to the east out of reach of the power of Rome and the eastern extremes of the Roman Empire —*Anatolia*, distant lands of Mesopotamia and Babylon and beyond to the Iranian plateau where the star-worshiper Zoroaster had once come preaching a belief that the multitude of divinities long held in awe by priests and peoples were but two primal forces of good and evil in constant combat for control over the natural and supernatural. The sorcerers devoted themselves to the good rather than the evil, and used their knowledge of the stars to predict events that served the former in opposition to the latter.

The sorcerers of Anatolia followed the star that guided them across the deserts, journeying in the wake of other nomadic travelers who centuries before had set out from Mesopotamia toward the land of Canaan. Unlike the first Hebrews led by Abraham, the sorcerers did not drive sheep and goats before them; but they were sufficiently wealthy to bring rich gifts of their lands: minerals and spices and ointments. They were uncertain of their destination, uncertain for whom the gifts were; they traveled with theirs eyes and ears open to any possibility to which the astral phenomenon might bring them. Passersby might wonder, "what folly is this, that sorcerers follow a strange star bringing rich gifts to where and to whom they know not?" The sorcerers had faith in their reading of the heavens, faith that the astral messenger was not bent on folly; something sensed and intuited informed them of the rectitude and certainty of their mission.

The sorcerers believed that the supernatural could interpose change and movement on the unchanging truths of the natural. The great certainty of the patterns of the heavens had meaning and influence over human events. The number of stars in the sky, the wandering planets, the patterns of the zodiac, held latent power, as did substances of the earth, air, fire, and water. The sorcerers, knowing that the divine and its many manifestations revealed truths to the willing observer, thinker, and listener, hurried them on in the conviction that without doubt the astral phenomena had supernatural origins, and must not be ignored.

The appearance of a star, a new light in the heavens, might signal any of a number of events. Time immemorial had taught prognosticators that stars were manifestations of the divine, even symbols of particular supernatural powers—to impregnate the barrenness of soil and womb with new life and growth, to stir among men the angst to desire power and conquer foes, to will to rise among others as king. This latter possibility, that an astral phenomenon was a supernatural sign of the birth of a king, quickened their step as they journeyed west.

It is not told how long was their journey and precisely from where they came; what were their names and nationalities; how many they were and whether or not they held political power among their respective peoples. The story of the sorcerers's journey to Palestine is anonymous about such details, but clear about their beliefs and purpose and about what they found when they arrived.

Ancient authorities on the practice of magic, who lived during the many centuries that the Roman Empire provided a unified structure for learning, believed that the magi, the sorcerers of Anatolia who were experts in astrology, divination, and magic, were opportunists. These Asian sorcerers claimed to be able to anticipate the interposition of the supernatural on the natural, to predict, anticipate, the arrival of divine hints of the future and read them when they arrived. Ancient scientists and philosophers were often incredulous about such claims, though they did not doubt the abilities of the sorcerers to use magic, to predict the future, and to gauge the will of heaven from the stars. Hence when the sorcerers from Anatolia crossed the Jordan River, entering into Palestine, following an astral phenomenon, their counterparts at the court of Herod, king of Judaea, sought to discover the magi's mission. Herod was like most ancient kings insecure in his power, wondering how long fate had decreed his rule, hungry to find out from any source, information about the future. He had court astrologers, to be sure—the strongest, wealthiest kings attracted the most skilled soothsayers, either Chaldean or trained by Chaldeans. Their positions at court, indeed their very lives, depended upon their skill at prognostication. The sorcerers arriving from the east were rivals, but could hardly be ignored.

Upon arriving at Jerusalem, the sorcerers went to the court of the king, whose name was Herod. Whether the king that they met with was Herod or his son and successor Herod Archelaus is unclear from the source, the *Gospel of Matthew*. The king and his advisers, upon learning of the coming of the magi from the east, following the sign of heaven, inquired of the sorcerers what they had seen and what it could mean. The sorcerers revealed enough of their mission to encourage speculation as to what the star could mean, but they were hesitant to put themselves into the hands of the king or his court astrologers. While the sorcerers stayed in Jerusalem an uncertain amount of time, they continued to see the astral phenomenon, and wondered when its true significance would be revealed.

The sorcerers either had learned beforehand or learned upon their arrival in Jerusalem that Jews were most particularly anxious about one future event, the coming of the anointed one, the Messiah. The Hebrews had for over a thousand years looked for the appearance of the anointed one, who would champion their cause, free them from suffering and political oppression, and lead them to a new age wherein the chosen people of Yahweh would find redemption and peace—and power and glory as well.

The yearning for a savior is common among individuals and

peoples throughout time. Some Hebrew writers, such as Isaiah, portrayed the Messiah as a "Prince of Peace," a humble and loving healer. The author of the Psalms believed the Messiah was Lord, son of God. Other Hebrew writers expected the Messiah to come in a blaze of glory. According to the author of the Old Testament book of Daniel, who wrote two to three hundred years before the reign of Herod, the Messiah would provide a temporal and secular manifestation of what all people seek, what people of the ancient world in particular sought: wealth, power, glory, revenge, martial success. More recently, perhaps only seventy years earlier, the writer Enoch had conceived of the Messiah as God's agent to avenge His enemies. Hence did the Jews hunger for the appearance of the *anointed one.*

Even if freed for short periods from the whims of rulers and soldiers, the people of Palestine, like most ancient peoples, were constantly pressured by famine, malnourishment, plague, individual illnesses, disability, insecurity, pain, and eventual death. Lives were short and brutish. Few people were educated, and most lived in fear of the unknown. Ignorance was the great ruler of all people, fed by the deception that life could be lived without pain, hunger, violence, and fear. People responded to their conditions by retreating inward to what was left of self, a dark, dismal region of absence of love and the ubiquity of pain and terror. The only release was death.

Out of the darkness a light shown. Hopeful individuals saw it, reached out to touch it, embrace it. Sin and despair often tried to cover the light, to smother its rays, to hide it though it could not be hidden. Somewhere the light still penetrated the darkness. The magi from Anatolia focused on the light amid the darkness of Herod's Judaea. As they viewed the suffering and poverty of the people and the lavish wealth and momentary power of the king and court; as they walked among religious leaders,

Pharisees and Sadducees and Essenes, who puffed themselves up thinking that they knew the will and ways of God; as they listened to astrologers and sorcerers who sought to tell the king what he wanted to hear—the magi still could see the light, the astral messenger that nightly appeared, giving them hope. So they waited. They knew that in time, soon, the astral messenger would reveal what they had journeyed so far to see. They waited in expectation of the supernatural.

7

PONDERING

Behold the handmaid of the Lord ...
Never has there been a more pure and holy place, one marked by God's love and will. It is a wilderness of utter security, warmth, and peace, an environment of darkness, stillness of time, space, and consciousness. There, in the womb, it is formed—all that is and will be, all that becomes, all that is living, breathing, knowing. In this prelude to consciousness is the conception of being. The womb holds timeless secrets revealed in time. A singular, eternal moment becomes flesh. The womb nurses the soul, the spirit, the essence, the mind, the feeling of oneness. In the unspoiled womb the supernatural becomes natural, and humanity is wrought from the divine. The tyranny of time and space is scarcely known in this nursery of grace.

> *For thou didst form my inward parts,*
> *Thou didst knit me together in my*
> *mother's womb.*

The Psalmist knew that the grandest moment in history is repeated over and over, worldwide, throughout time. Everywhere conception and pregnancy result in new life, in the thoughts and ideas of the parents made flesh, the spirit of endeavor, love, and survival breathing, crying, reaching out in love, receiving love. The incarnation occurs, the child is born, its origins unknown, the miracle of its conception unexplained, the path it shall take undetermined, the will through which it shall act unformed. An image of the divine, sweet purity unperturbed, unstained by evil, profile of truth, fresh and new, content in grace, by angelic care secured, a gift by which the will of God is served.

Repeatedly the mother is asked to accept the burden of the creation and nurturing of life. Repeatedly she is asked to risk her peace and contentment, to give herself to another, to sacrifice self for another, to become two when she has been one, to break from selfishness and her supposed singularity to sponsor new life, to nurture the divine. Her natural impulse is to resist. Who can accept the call to pain, sacrifice, and suffering? How can she accept the endless torment of fear, the anxiety of self made manifold in another? Why must she accept what is not her will? Why must she accept her destiny? Her hesitancy gives way to something within telling her to accept.

The child is blessed from the moment of conception. The blessed being is given the vast riches of life. He is blessed as well with the intuitive feelings of love. He is a seeker and receiver of love, which is as much as anyone can ask for in life. Life's setting, events, duration, pleasure and pain, matter little: for he is blessed with *life*. He has a mind with which to think, to reason and calculate who he is. The surroundings in which he lives provide him ample opportunities with which to search for the truth, and abide by it accordingly. This truth is not outside of him anyway, yet always in him, even before birth. There, in the womb, *he is*.

The blessed being is as pure as his circumstances allow. Sin as a product of willfulness is a present unknown possible only in the future. Life brings movement, pain, frustration, growth, illness, and the ever present chance of death. Such is original sin. The infant will respond to his physical needs and cry in hunger. Yet his spiritual innocence is unsurpassed. He is created in God's image; hence he is goodness itself; he is love; he is and was and will be.

Life is a search to recapture the oneness and grace of the womb. After birth, all forward movement is looking backward. The very nature of sin is the feeling of being incomplete, the insecurity, the dissatisfaction with self all alone with self. One person, twisted by hate and bitterness, lashes out against others in violence; another seeks to acquire more material goods; yet another yearns for unending euphoria and pleasure—all are panaceas to loneliness, despair, self-hatred, rejection. The power of dominance, the illusory hubris of riches, the excitement of the narcissistic moment brought about by intoxication, are feeble attempts to regain the contentment, warmth, and utter love of the womb. The future is utterly beholden to the past in the fruitless search to recapture the bliss of conception.

Mother will swaddle the child in love, clothe him in hope, and pray that he will live forever just as he is, running, laughing, playing, singing—a flowing and vibrant lump of clay fashioned into the most beautiful sculpture of God's utter and complete benevolence. For mother, the blessed child will be a constant reminder of unborn life, the hidden seed, the pinpoint of light thriving with the promise of life, marked by God, known to God, yet unseen by humans, unknown to anyone save the mother. The father will see in it over and over the miracle of birth, emerging from the dark silence of the womb into the consciousness of noise and light, the mother's screams and the babe's cries combining to form a mystical symphony to be played repeatedly throughout the ages. Few experiences are more ubiquitous than mother and child living a lullaby of daily life. The mother treasures these experiences in her heart.

In the womb the blessed child consciously begins to form his environment. The material world succumbs to its power. An idea has been born, a human the likes of which has never been seen, the power to live unsurpassed, its ability to mirror the transcendent inherent, its urge to love unquenchable, its thirst to know unstoppable, its instinctual drive for peace, contentment, silence, humility, and acceptance pervasive.

Yet the blessed being emerges into a world of ignorance and darkness, where all that *is* becomes dominated by fears of what will be and anxieties about what has been. Time curses this being and shrouds the meaning of life in a mist of momentary, corporeal, fleeting, transient, concerns. All that seems to matter does not. All that appears significant is not. Life itself, and the divine spark within it, is the buried core to all else that flutters and blows about making noise and causing terror.

The child was conceived when the world hungered for the divine embrace, for love that would be eternal. The world had had enough of hate to inspire this urge for the peace and bliss of the divine. Priests and prophets, holy men and women, offered a route to, communication with, the transcendent ideas and forces of life, love, and nature. There were mysteries that only a few wise people knew; they formed ceremonies and sacraments for the uninitiated to become initiated into the secrets of the divine. So many were the possibilities! Each place had a favorite, some heavenly being to answer needs and reward behavior. The deities went by different names, donned different apparel, enjoyed special powers, and were particularly jealous of rivals. The Egyptian fertility goddess Isis, the Thracian god of ecstasy Dionysus, the Earth Mother Cybele, the Sun god Mithras, the divine singer holding the keys to the underworld Orpheus, the divine healer Asclepius, had rites of initiation that led to a mystical cleansing of sin, which resulted in communion with the divine to transcend the body, time, and evil—the result would be eternal joy.

The mysteries remained mysterious, and only the dead knew the truth. How often do the living know the truth? Did Mary know the truth? Did the ethereal messenger from God implant not only the seed of God, the Son, but commensurate knowledge as well? The Apostle Luke thought as much.

Mary pondered in her heart the gift of the child. Pondering, feeling, sensing: God chose Mary for her empathy, her talent at pondering life, feeling another's feelings, sensing human character. Life is countless people each with an infinite number of potential experiences all interacting and being experienced simultaneously. God in a single moment, as Aurelius Augustine argued, peruses the whole of experience, the infinite plethora of human experiences. God's perusal is empathetic; God feels all of these human experiences. Empathy in the singular moment connects with transcendence of human experience. When Mary pondered in her heart she experienced this empathetic transcendence, feeling and sensing the manifold experiences that her child would enjoy and endure over his life. This empathetic transcendence occurs in a single moment of awareness, an entrance to the transcendent truth that is God. Isolated human experiences combine into a whole, into a united human experience that transcends the individual moment. Her response to the miraculous, to the improbable circumstances of her life and the child's conception, was understanding, simple humility, and acceptance of God's will.

8

A CHILD IS BORN

And shepherds were tending their sheep at night and behold . . . The grinding movement of time toward the end was slow and steady, one day following another, night falling expectantly, darkness ruling the land until the hues of dawn foretold the beginning of a new day like all the others. The beauties of starry nights and rosy dawns were lost amid the suffering and cries of the tortured, ill, and dying. The people could not see that truth and goodness overshadowed the land at dusk and brightened the world with new light. The divine punctuated the sameness of daily toil and disturbed repose. Creation waited expectantly, if humans were blind to the emerging truth surrounding them. The stars appeared ever brighter, the night sky ever clearer, the sounds of night like a choir rejoicing in the arrival of the child. Most people closed their doors and shuttered their windows to the lights and sounds of the night. Some people, however, could not help but see and hear. Shepherds watching over their flocks knew the night sky, watched the progression of stars and constellations, kept track of Orion and the Pleiades, the rising of the Dog Star, Sirius, the strange patterns of the wandering planets. They knew the sounds of night, and the sameness of each night, the constancy of creation from season to season. But there was a change to the unending sameness. The constancy of nature was suspended as the timeless entered time. The lights and songs of the night jarred them from their slumber, and they looked in awe, listened intently, to the message told them by the night. *A child is born. God is with you.*

Travelers caught on the road took extra care to keep to the path, letting the stars, which shown brightly in the clear desert air, guide them. Gentle zephyrs whispered among the palms, sycamores, and figs. Those still awake resting after the labors of the day awaited sleep and the new day. Everyone, human and beast, anticipated dawn. In the town, a few feeble lights interrupted the overwhelming darkness. Candlelight and oil lamps cast great shadows upon mothers caring for sick children, feeble old men refusing to sleep, and the anxious despairing over deeds of the past and retribution yet to come. Tavern owners had shut the doors and hostelers closed the gates. Those wanderers needing food and rest were left to fend for themselves.

The man and woman, having come from afar to fulfill the requirements of the law, arrived after dark. The man was a native of the town, though not a resident, and had known of neither friends nor family who could host him and the woman for the night. The woman was exhausted and about to give birth. Starlight pointed the way to a rustic barn filled with hay and feeding troughs. The woman tried to stifle her fears and the cries of pain as the baby would wait no longer. The man found a bucket and a well, drew water and wet some clothes, and tended the woman the best he could. After a time she made the final push and the baby emerged in a splash of warm fluid from the womb amid cries of anguish and joy. The man cut the cord and gave the naked child to the mother, who wrapped him in clothes to protect him from the cold and held him to her still heaving breast. Soon the cries were stifled and the child slept. The man put the child in the only object resembling a cradle, a manger that he packed with straw. The woman kneaded her womb to try to stop the ongoing cramps.

In the dead of night the stars shown more brightly, particularly one that seemed to herald for the man the new life brought into the world. Accompanying the apparent brightening of the star were noises caused by the movement of the natural and supernatural. The man heard rapturous singing voices and wondered whence they came. Soon he heard the footsteps and shouts of man, and guardedly asked what they wanted. He could detect trembling in their voices and fear in their faces, glistening from tears. They were shepherds, they said, who were reclining in the surrounding hills, watching over their sheep, when they had been astonished by amazing figures in the sky, glowing ethereally, singing, glorifying God. One of the messengers told them of the miraculous birth of the son of the most high God in this very town of Bethlehem, and that the child would be found lying in a manger in a barn. When the messengers departed, in their wake was the bright starlight that shown upon the town. The men said that though they had been terrified they could not doubt their senses, and knew that God had commanded them to go and find the baby, to worship this child, Immanuel. They looked upon the sleeping infant and continued to weep and shutter excitedly, glorifying God and the great miracle He had deigned to allow them to witness.

The appearance of the shepherds astonished Joseph, the father, who was nevertheless not completely unprepared. He was a descendant of King David, the anointed, and had been taught the Scripture, and knew the prophecies that the Messiah would herald from the house of David, and be born in the City of David, Bethlehem, Joseph's own birthplace. Although Joseph was a craftsman, not a scholar, he was dutiful in attending the synagogue, following Mosaic Law, and reading the Scriptures. He knew what Isaiah said about the suffering servant who would be born of a virgin. Reality and experience reflected the dream that had informed Joseph that his wife, Mary, was this virgin.

Mary listened to the shepherds and pondered what they had witnessed. All that she had been told was coming true. Nine months before, she had been a young maiden living with her parents in Nazareth in Galilee, betrothed to a good man, Joseph the carpenter. Her dreamlike experience of the messenger who hailed her and proclaimed that she was the mother of God had in due course occurred as predicted: her body had changed and her womb had grown. The birth of a wonderful, healthy child and the words of the shepherds were amazing, if expected.

Joseph and Mary had bound themselves in the acceptance of God's will. During Mary's pregnancy they had learned, along with the other inhabitants of Galilee, Samaria, and Judaea, of Caesar's requirement that all heads of family enroll at the place of their birth. Mary had been in her ninth month when they began the five-day journey to Bethlehem. Jews were taught to obey the Mosaic Law in synagogue and the Roman law by circumstance.

The checkered political history of the Jews, the ongoing political struggle for power by dynasts among the chosen people, combined with the ceaseless aggression directed toward Israel and Judah, later Galilee, Samaria, and Judaea, by outsiders—Chaldeans, Assyrians, Persians, Greeks, Romans—had left the Jews a weakened people subject to the whims of outside forces. For several generations the most compelling and dominant force was that of Rome. Like most occupying powers throughout history, Rome required little from its subject peoples as long as they obeyed the laws and paid their taxes. The enrollment that forced Joseph and Mary to journey to Bethlehem was in accord with the latter. Romans governed subject peoples indirectly by means of local rulers, kings and tyrants, and directly, by appointed officials, who were given complete authority subject to the supervision of the Senate, formerly, and at this time, the imperial power, held by Octavian, or Augustus, Caesar. Augustus, the adopted son of Julius Caesar, had held power for almost forty years. He along with other tyrants, had destroyed the Republic, substituting the rule of one person. Augustus held power by controlling Rome's huge military. In the Near East, he preferred to control kingdoms by means of a patron-client relationship with rulers such as Herod and his sons and successors. These men ruled as long as they followed Augustus' bidding and kept order. Often they worked in cooperation with Roman officials—procurators, propraetors, proconsuls, and governors. Augustus maintained remarkable control by a strong Roman troop presence on the frontiers of an empire that encompassed parts of three continents. The large military was a continual drain on the empire's resources, for which Augustus paid by taxation. To know what was the proper tax quota for each province and client kingdom required meticulous records of the number of citizens. Hence Augustus ordered the enrollment, or census.

Joseph, Mary, and the child stayed in Bethlehem for several days to allow for Mary's recovery and for Joseph to enroll with the local officials. Joseph was able to find more secure lodgings for his family. He prepared to make the journey home to Nazareth, planning on his way to stop at Jerusalem to accomplish Mary's purification according to Mosaic Law and for the circumcision of the child according to the Abrahamic Covenant. Meanwhile the shepherds were not silent about their miraculous experience. Word had spread and the devout and curious came from surrounding villages to see the child. Most astonishing of all the visitors were Chaldean stargazers bearing gifts and kneeling before the child.

9

HIDDEN YEARS

T*he child grew, and waxed strong in spirit...* The childhood and adolescence of Jesus of Nazareth are hidden years. About his own life, Jesus had little to say. From indirect sources we learn about his life and times. These sources, the writings of Matthew, Mark, Luke, John, the Apostle Paul, Thomas, and the Jewish historian Josephus, are obscure in either origin, authorship, or veracity. The debate over the quality and truth of these sources has been intense, occupying centuries of claims and counterclaims. The argument ranges from total acceptance, at least of those sources that make up the New Testament, that the Gospels and Epistles of Paul are little short of the word of God; to those on the opposite extreme who claim that these writings are a fabrication. In between are more sober commentaries that assess these writings for what they clearly are —biographical and evocative accounts of the life and teachings of a man who inspired these writers sufficiently that they at least believed that what they recorded was an accurate portrayal of the truth. Moreover, there is a moral and existential truth to the Gospels eliciting from the reader a subjective response.

If Joseph, in response to a dream, took the child and his wife to Egypt to escape Herod's wrath, as Matthew claims, then Jesus would have glimpsed firsthand the place from which Moses led the children of Israel, as recounted in the *Book of Exodus*. Egypt like all of the Mediterranean region had been dominated by the Roman Empire for several centuries. The Roman rise to power had been rapid and ruthless. The Romans had conquered Carthage in North Africa in a series of Punic Wars and had obliterated the city of Carthage itself. During the second century, *Ante Christos*, the Romans had invaded Greece, conquering Macedon and its king Philip V, followed by western Asia, conquering the Seleucid Empire, a large Greek empire that was the remnant of the conquests of Alexander the Great. The varied wars that resulted in Roman power led to squabbling among powerful generals, the most famous of whom, Julius Caesar, attempted to establish himself as a king in the mid first century. Caesar's rule was short-lived, however, as he was assassinated in 44 *Ante Christos*, which began a conflict between Octavian (Augustus) Caesar and Mark Antony and his lover Cleopatra, queen of Egypt. Octavian marched on and occupied Egypt in 31. Egypt was Octavian's personal province during his long reign of forty-five years. If Joseph and his family fled to Egypt to escape the power of Herod, they could not escape the overwhelming dominance of Rome. Perhaps, depending on how long the family resided in Egypt, Jesus learned of the Septuagint, the Greek Old Testament, and was influenced by the sophisticated cosmopolitan Hellenistic culture, which had existed in Egypt for three hundred years, centered in the city of Alexandria.

At some point Joseph brought his family back to Judaea, following the dictates of a dream, and moved on to Nazareth, again in accordance with a dream. There he and Mary and the child lived. If Joseph and Mary took Jesus with them on an annual journey from Galilee to Judaea for the Passover, then perhaps Luke's story is true that when Jesus was twelve years old he broke from his parent's supervision for several days, spending his time at the Temple questioning the Pharisees and Sadducees, the scholars of the Torah and the Law, asking difficult questions and posing remarkable answers. To engage in a dialogue with such men would require a person who was a great thinker, but also someone who had been educated in Jewish traditions and holy scriptures, someone who could read and write. Matthew and Luke express the incredulity of the people of Nazareth at Jesus's learning when he was, after all, only a carpenter's son. Joseph's pride in his lineage of the House of David made him a man of scripture able to impart his knowledge of law, history, prophets, and stories, to his son.

Mostly Jesus's early years are hidden. These were generative years, years of discovery and assimilation, of planning and fulfillment, when ideas emerge and are tested against experience. These were years of the question, which is the starting point of the seeker. The interrogative in human existence springs from the complete and utter loneliness of the individual thinker, the primordial core of self, the deep and hidden recess of experience and intuitive awareness of being. The question emerges from experience naked, devoid of moral systems, certainties, truths, standards, culture. The question yields fear of the unknown, of ignorance, of loneliness, as the seeker stares with wide-eyed wonder into the infinite of the universe.

The *terra incognita* of the human mind, the unknown of the temporal, intellectual, emotional, and spiritual, is great. But each person has a personal journey, an internal necessity that demands movement, the search within to the realm of the personal past as well as extension outward into the future from the basis of the past. During such times of searching one learns of self, who one is and what one does, what should be the direction amid the possible paths. It is an age of self-discovery. One finds within some inner strength that is one's essence, one's mind, one's being.

As during the night storm lightning flashes brilliantly, momentarily revealing things, so the intuitive flash of insight reveals, if but for an instant, all things. A voice cries in the wilderness of silence. The call is the unmistakable presence of being, a streak of light amid the limbs and branches of the towering forest of darkness, doubt, will, and narcissism. A violent wind courses through the hills and valleys: but whence does it come, to where does it go? One feels its presence and knows its power.

God is a feeling more than a thought, is experienced not reasoned. The child feels God, knows God, better, more deeply, than does the philosopher, whose cogitations lead to theories and absurdities that contradict God's true being. Is love rational? God is that great feeling of warmth, yearning, and attachment—and fear, too, of the end of attachment, which cements love ever greater. The child feels the passage of time, feels the great unknown, feels the questions and possible answers of life, feels the simple truths of warmth, father's hugs and mother's kisses, the wonders of the night sky, a full stomach. The child feels God. But time intervenes, and the arrogance of reason, so that few adolescents or adults feel God in the way they once did, when young, innocent, pure, godlike—a blessed being.

Humans over the course of time, individually and as a group, become aware of self, that *I am*. The child senses the *other* and tries to mold his environment to fit his own needs. Frustration grows with each step, each accomplishment—for there are so many other challenges that wait! Necessities slowly separate from possibilities, which grow in number, subject to particular actions of manipulation. The blessed child begins to notice in possibility, plurality, and multiplicity the vastness and wonder of the universe. At some point in the young life a vague awareness of the mystery of the Creation yields a recognition of "my light and my truth," God.[1] The child listens to the sublime music of creation and hears the voice of the Creator. He stirs to the harmonies, chords, and choruses of the choir of being. He yearns to add his song to the whole, to sing aloud of himself. The voice of the divine wells up within him, demanding release. He sings:

> O Lord, thou hast searched me and known me!
> Thou knowest when I sit down and when I rise up;
> Thou discernest my thoughts from afar.
> Thou searchest out my path and my lying down,
> And art acquainted with all my ways.
> Even before a word is on my tongue,
> Lo, O Lord, thou knowest it altogether.
> Thou dost beset me behind and before.
> And layest thy hand upon me.
> Such knowledge is too wonderful for me;
> It is high, I cannot attain it.

The blessed child is completely absorbed with love, peace, and contentment. Daily life teaches him these truths. The fluffy clouds of sunny days, brush-strokes in the sky, are a symbol of the warmth and softness of life in the womb of nature. Pillow dreams of white swans floating, peaceful armies dressed in white marching, and cottontails bounding through the woods of deep blue dominate thoughts and feelings. In the cradle of nature the aura of love drips from trees on a cool autumn day in the forest, the swaying branches singing a lullaby to the sleepy child within, the leaves floating gently to the ground, falling in accord to a higher will, covering the seeds of future growth. The wisdom and words of nature teach the willing youth who responds with prayerful piety to the seas, mountains, forests, deserts, and plains:

> 'T is elder Scripture, writ by God's own hand,-
> Scripture authentic! Uncorrupt by man.[2]

Such truth simply overwhelms the child, and he sees himself in nature's spiritual mirrors: meaning takes on flesh.

The scripture of nature teaches the child the ethical codes of goodness and benevolence that reflect the light of the universe—

> To me still speaks Thy voice, myself I see,
> I see myself in each new scene reveal'd.[3]

—that others besides himself have the same wonder as the stars, the same warmth as the sun, the same attraction as the pleasant meadow, the same beauty as flowers in bloom, all a miracle in their own right, derived from one and the same source. The child learns that morality contains but one law, to respond piously to such wonder with love toward others and oneself.

The blessed being finds the lessons of nature a complete study, the appendices of which come from the minds of humankind. The mountains and the seas, rivers and valleys, rain and soil, sources of life, yield thoughts of purpose, goodness, and love. The child knows from simple empathy with the creation what few sages know from the study of books—that life's greatest lesson is acceptance and humility, to give into a higher will, to live passively in the present moment rather than actively searching the forgotten past or anticipating the uncertain future.

> The divine will is a deep abyss
> of which the present moment is the entrance.[4]

The abyss encompasses human time, a great horizontal valley between two distant summits the vertical heights of which are infinite. All is a mystery, the spiritual route of the ascent to the unseen summit as well as the events spanning the valley. One's steps are "mere drops" in "an ocean of midnight darkness." Easy it is to drown. What knowledge does the past yield that cannot be found in the present moment? Such is the irony of history, that it tempts us to inquire into a vanished nothingness of *what was* for the sake of confronting the comparable nothingness of *what will be*. Into this abyss the blessed child journeyed.

Awareness of time accompanies awareness of self. But time "is never still"; if only one's mind "could be seized and held steady" one "short moment" one "would glimpse the splendour of eternity which is for ever still."[5] Happiness is elusive because of time's never-ending fluidity. Hence could one poet conclude:

> All things are full of weariness;
> A man cannot utter it;
> The eye is not satisfied with seeing,
> Nor the ear filled with hearing.
> What has been is what will be,
> And what has been done is what will be done;
> And there is nothing new under the sun.

Meaninglessness, according to *Ecclesiastes*, follows close upon the experience of time. Why is there such restlessness, such dependence on the passing moment, such a narcissistic search for constant gratification, that bards and sages pass on their doubts and fears through their thoughts and verse? Yet time cannot destroy teachings that transcend the ages.

The wisdom of the past counsels acceptance. The Hebrew poets called upon their listeners to end resistance and to recognize that "all is vanity," to realize that "he who increases knowledge increases sorrow." One's only response is to "fear God, and keep his commandments," to "cast your burden on the Lord, and he will sustain you." "For God alone my soul waits in silence," wrote the Psalmist, "for my hope is from him. He only is my rock and my salvation, my fortress; I shall not be shaken."

To live is to experience fear. A child's fear is a response to the uncertainty of his environment—the constant possibility of loneliness, the darkness of night, the unknown, pain. But ever balancing fear is love.

There is no fear in love, but perfect love casts out fear.

Love removes torment, yields the blessing of stillness and silence, to know at this and every moment the presence of that which transcends, yet is fully encompassed in, the moment. There is much a child does not understand. But he knows love, which is sufficient, knowledge itself.

10

DECEIVER

Go behind me, Satan . . .
The further the distance in time of the child's journey from the womb, the more overwhelming becomes sin—ignorance, pain, selfishness, suffering, temporality, corporeality, temptation, error, and death—which is inherent in human existence. Sin is a stain, the soiling agent of which is life.

The journey from childhood to adulthood yields a discovery of the curse and the blessing of life. Contradiction follows upon growth and change: action and passivity intertwine, as does knowledge and ignorance, certainty and doubt.

> I seem to wander through mysterious ways,
> Shadows of other days.[1]

Euphoria and depression, health and sickness, poverty and wealth, concern and apathy: the temptation toward opposites and contradictions greets each passing moment. Free choice is the way of life, which is of one path and its many shadows. It takes a clear light to discover reality amid deception. Evil haunts the good and preys, as it were, on the unsuspecting wayfarer lost in thoughts of future conquests and past wonders, enthralled with momentary pleasures that intoxicate and cause one to forget the responsibility of following the one rule of life. A person fears the future, fears what they are and will remain or become, fears boredom, fears pain, fears death. Momentary pleasure, momentary glory, momentary satisfaction of hunger, can stifle the pain, the fear of the future, if just for a moment. The seductiveness of momentary pleasure rids one temporarily of the constant overwhelming fear of life. Ignorance and forgetfulness, the search for pleasure and avoidance of pain, are weak pleas when truth embraces one's whole being. Purposeful will to err against the blessedness of one's own life as well as others is sin indeed.

Sin fascinates humans because of its ubiquity throughout time. Sin is the stuff of history because its counterpart, goodness, is such a rare phenomenon—at least in history books. Stories of goodness gather dust on bookshelves; it is the stories of sin that are read again and again. "All men in the state of nature have a desire and will to hurt," declared Thomas Hobbes in *Leviathan*; "we must therefore resolve, that the original of all great and lasting societies consisted not in the mutual good will men had towards each other, but in the mutual fear they had of each other." With such an argument the English philosopher Hobbes said that humans must be terrified into good behavior. And yet temptation comes again in the wake of the passing storm.

Temptation manifests itself as a subtle, probing fear linked to all that one is not, all that contradicts self, all that is out of reach. The corporeal tempts with images of grandeur, power, beauty, wealth, wisdom, all "things of a day" in Aeschylus's words, passing fancies, neither lasting nor of any spiritual depth—rather like humans. Knowledge, immortality, independence, control, and security are tauntingly out of reach, yet implanted in the imagination as possible to attain. When success is elusive, when realization of impossibility briefly surfaces, fear grips with the utter reality of ignorance, dependence, powerlessness, insecurity, and death. The recognition of the irreversibility of death is the true source of temptation. To escape death is to escape temptation, hence to escape sin.

The sting of death is sin.

Why would one err but for the ubiquitous presence of mortality? Merely by living—that is, slowly dying—one sins. The blessed being cannot help but sin, cannot resist temptation.

The human struggle against temptation is unending. The intellect and the ability to solve the problems of self and others tempt with the invitation that all problems will give way to solutions, all questions find an answer. Yet the answer and the solution are insignificant without the question and the problem. What is the beauty of health without sickness? Who can heal without disease? So one heals, grateful for both the malady and the cure. The challenge of the cure is to accept its limitation as a temporary stopgap amid a continual process of disintegration. No cure is *permanent*. The events of a person's history, whether of the body or the mind, are rarely controllable. Nor are the events of the external world subject to the individual will.

The blessed man learns as he gains experience to resist the temptation to try to will what is not his to will, to control what is not his to control. He learns surrender, acceptance, humility, obedience. His mother and father, his birthplace, the events of his childhood, are not his to control. His calling, his work, his gifts, are given not acquired. The duration of his life, whether or not his death is lasting and painful, are not in his hands. All that he controls is his ability to achieve contentment notwithstanding the circumstances of the intricate, multitudinous moments of his life.

The blessed man is the voice of one who cries in the wilderness: the voice of the soul, the self who knows what is true, who recognizes temptation and fear, and calls out to all to accept fear and self and to break from the deceptions of the moment, which only forestall the ultimate coming to terms with God.

Jesus, like his cousin John (the Baptist), was a wanderer in the mountains of the Holy Land. He often felt that there was no place to lay his head because of the challenge of the wilderness: the desert of the mind and the thorn of the flesh, the thirst for peace and truth, the hot dry wind of sin's oppression on the mind, the blinding truth of the sun the heat and brightness of which he constantly sought escape by finding the peace of shade and cool waters, the oasis that provides momentary relief from the challenges to one's mind and body. It takes tremendous will to break from the cool waters and fresh fruit of the oasis to continue the journey into the heat and privation of the wilderness of life, where is found emptiness, doubt, uncertainty, and barrenness. The challenge is to fill the emptiness and barrenness, to fill with the fullness and plenty of life, the certainty of faith, the bedrock of hope.

Physician, heal thyself: it is one thing to know and another to practice knowledge. The wilderness of time and life brought about manifold temptations, deception. When he was at his weakest, the deceiver came to him, offering a solution to fear, insecurity, powerlessness, doubt—a solution to living in the moment. The deceiver offered power, conquering death, satisfying the appetite, embracing fame.

The people of the first century, *Anno Domini*, personified evil and deception with the image of satan (*satanas*), the devil (*diabolos*), literally the *accuser*: enemy, traducer, seducer, deceiver.² Satan is the deceiver, and anyone who similarly falls into his trap of lies, mis-truths, and hiding, is a deceiver, too. The deceiver acts like everything is right even when it is not. The deceiver deceives everyone, including himself. The deceiver knows what is right and wrong but can deceive himself or others that the wrong is right. The deceiver will come up with any explanation or logic to defend or convince himself or others of his rectitude. The deceiver is a coward, afraid, because he does not want anyone to know who he really is or what he really does. He puts on an act and facade, hiding his true feelings, his fears, his actions, terrified that they will be discovered and his cover as a deceiver will be blown. A deceiver can distort reality anytime he wants it to fit his designs, or to accomplish his ultimate goal of masking his fears, that is, inundating his pain with the elusiveness of temporary pleasure. If one successfully deceives then there is a brief relief or pleasure in putting off the truth, in hiding once again. What happens in the present moment is all that matters to the deceiver. What has been shown false in the past is forgotten. What might happen in the future is unimportant, indeed fearsome, hence best to put it off with more deception. What the deceiver most fears is that without deception, the real person will emerge, and what if the real person is not what he wishes it to be? What is the real person, anyway—what is the person in all nakedness, an open book, all his insecurities and fears and self-loathing open for all to see? Best to hide, to deceive, both oneself and others. But God knows.

Jesus, the blessed man, was constantly tempted by the deceiver, not just in the physical state of wilderness but the wilderness that is life. Time and again people deceived, seduced, and tempted, and he had to respond, as he did to his closest disciple Peter, "Go behind me, Satan, because you have in mind not the things of God but the things of men."[3] Satan is anyone who doubts and denies the truth, a person who deceives himself and others into thinking about self, saving oneself, to overwhelm reason with awe and wonder, to mystify, to grab the senses, to convince otherwise, to kidnap the mind and body, to imprison one's sense of normality, one's sense of rightness and goodness. To deceive is to seduce with evil. But to be seduced and to allow it, not to resist, is evil too. To be seduced and to allow it is a way to become a seducer. Seduction involves an *other*, an outside force, who seeks to impose its will on one's own will. This imposition is malevolent in nature, an attempt to capture, take over, conquer. A seducer, a deceiver, is therefore an invader of another person's freedom, privacy, reason, feelings, and sense of self.

Satan attempts to seduce humans, as he attempted to seduce Jesus, with fear. For over a thousand years, *Ante Christos*, the Hebrews experienced this seduction and deception. The history of the children of Israel was one of wandering, of avoiding, of fearing, of replacing truth with idols: anything that directed them away from the reality of God, embracing a substitute truth that is not truth, rather an easy alternative that allowed them to put themselves in its embrace, but all the while it was deceptive, a figment of the imagination, a falsehood, a temporary fix, a fantasy. Hebrews worshiped idols as a replacement for the truth of God because they gave into their fears of the moment, and idols provided a fantasy to replace fear in the passing moments.

But love knows no fear. Jesus rejected the seduction of the deceiver by embracing his fears, of pain, mortality, life: to accept fear is to accept self. It is to give in—Jesus gave in, to God, to love. With God, whom should I fear? Humans do not realize that the deceiver, the evil to fear most, is not outside of us, but within us. If we can accept our fears, accept ourselves, then outside events are not as fearful. To conquer fear in oneself is to conquer fear elsewhere. Jesus had no fear of man or institutions or Satan or wilderness or self. He had only fear of God, that is, he humbly accepted the will of God, and did not give into his fears of sin and death, but by accepting God's will, accepted sin and death.

Love works in time and so it will be imperfect and never absolute. Love is not a metaphysical, rather an emotional, physical, and psychic reality in time. Likewise evil is not transcendent, but found in the everyday temptations of life. Love is therefore a historical process in each *year of our Lord*. Love is found in the moment as well as in the transcendent. God's will is revealed through His love, which is both transcendent and everyday. Jesus rejected Satan by accepting and willingly responding to God's love, conforming to His will. He exercised free will within the confines of God's grace.

This is my beloved Son, in whom I am well pleased.

III

TRANSFIGURATION

Transformed by the renewing of your minds.

11

TIMELESS ENTERS TIME

And he was transfigured before them...

Ancient humans, living before the time when humans embraced the scientific mentality such that they convinced themselves that they were sovereign over nature rather than the other way around, felt that nature was alive, filled with spirits, with life, both physical and spiritual. Ancient humans conceived of a relationship of the transcendent and transient, the divine and corporeal, that has become foreign, ludicrous, to the skeptical incredulity of our present age. The Roman poet Ovid summed the ancient awareness, even expectation, that the timeless interacts with time when in his *Metamorphoses* he wrote that in the beginning, at the creation, "forms are changed into new bodies," such that the "Artificer of all things" forms humans "from divine elements."[1] Ovid called this *metamorphosis*. Philo Judaeus, the Jewish philosopher of the first century, *Anno Domini*, echoed Ovid, writing: "The elements are inanimate matter, and immovable by any power of their own, being subjected to the operator on them to receive from him every kind of shape or distinctive quality which he chooses to give them."[2]

Another ancient writer likewise wrote an account of metamorphosis in a story about *The Golden Ass*. Lucius Apuleius, living during the second century, *Anno Domini*, spun a tale of a hapless man transformed by magic into a four-legged ass. What appears to be a humorous tale of the credulity of the ancients to believe in witches and enchantments becomes something much more. Apuleius tells of a man who goes through such suffering and fear, as a human and as an ass, that he is finally through prayer metamorphosized into a life of peace and contentment. This is by means of the intervention of the transcendent, symbolized by Isis, the Egyptian fertility goddess, into the man's life. Isis represents the fundamental deity, of which there are many manifestations. Isis is the light and truth, very similar to the *Logos* of ancient Greek philosophy—and very similar to the Christian concept of Christ the Logos. The cult of Isis was like many such ancient cults restricted to adherents who went through the necessary secret sacraments, which revealed the nature of the divine. Conversion was a *metamorphosis* of a person to realize and accept the transcendent. Apuleius told the story of Cupid and Psyche to illustrate the transcendent connection of the divine to the transient human, as characterized by Love (Cupid) and Soul (Psyche). Love comes to Soul, but hesitantly, and Soul does not quite know Love. Soul suffers, feels a distance from Love. But eventually Soul and Love are united and spend life in eternity.[3]

Logos—the eternal truth made manifest in the human mind in thoughts and words—was an idea with a long history in the ancient world. For centuries ancient philosophers speculated on the nature of *logos*. It fit perfectly well with the metaphysics of Plato as well as the Stoic belief in a universal benevolence, a divine spirit of which all humans are a part. The Greeks were lovers of grand ideas, and though there were Skeptics, and materialists such as the Epicureans, few Greeks doubted that there was some core idea, a spiritual center, a universal and absolute force defined by early philosophers such as Xenophanes as the *mind*, or to Parmenides the *one*, or the *universal soul* according to Pythagoras, or to Anaximander of Miletus, the *infinite*. The *logos* simply *is*.

The Stoics, such as Zeno, Seneca, and Epictetus, embraced the *logos*, the *transcendent utterance*, and built a philosophy of peace and love upon it. Philo Judaeus, one of the most extensive ancient writers of the concept, declared that God creates not over time, but "at once, not merely by uttering a command, but by even thinking of it." Philo believed that the logos was known even to Hebrew philosophers. Moses was well versed in Egyptian philosophy, hence knew that there had to be "an active cause, and a passive subject; and that the active cause is the intellect of the universe, thoroughly unadulterated and thoroughly unmixed, superior to virtue and superior to science, superior even to abstract good or abstract beauty; while the passive subject is something inanimate and incapable of motion by an intrinsic power of its own, but having been set in motion, and fashioned, and endowed with life by the intellect, became transformed into that most perfect work, this world."[4]

Even warriors and kings could partake of the idea. Marcus Aurelius, for example, was a Stoic philosopher whom fate had thrust into a position of utter responsibility as leader of a state of millions of people. During his reign as emperor of Rome, from 161 to 180, *Anno Domini*, the Roman Empire suffered military disasters and plague. Aurelius found himself usually not in Rome but encamped on the Danube River facing Germanic invaders. That Stoicism taught human equality and the brotherhood of humankind was not lost on Aurelius, who resented his military duties and ruminated about the nature and meaning of life. He based his ideas of the brevity and insignificance of life, the irrelevance of fame and glory, and the ignorance and depravity of humanity, on the contemplation of his own thought and experiences in light of the thoughts and experiences of other, past humans. He perceived existence in terms of the present as a moment in time. But this awareness was based not on a restricted perception of time and existence, rather on a broad perspective, to the degree that Aurelius could conceive of one's life as a solitary moment amid the many moments that make up existence as a whole. "In the life of a man, his time is but a moment." Life for Aurelius was a continuum of movement from past to future, a seamless process, a flowing, the stops or moments of which reduce to nothingness. Whereas another might see one's life as an end in itself, Aurelius understood life as just a moment in something much greater, something incomprehensible. As just a moment in time, the duration of life is insignificant. "Were you to live three thousand years, or even thirty thousand, remember that the sole life which a man can lose is that which he is living at the moment.... This means that the longest life and the shortest amount to the same thing."[5]

Grappling with mortality, with fear brought upon him by the responsibility of the imperial throne, Aurelius counseled, cajoled, talked with himself by means of *Meditations*. He lived each moment, "every one of life's experiences," trying to gauge "its worth to the universe," to the whole. Believing that in the "present moment" is found "all that has been since time began, and all that shall be unto the world's end," seeing "virtue" as a transcending force, he tried to cultivate "the divine spirit within me" to achieve such virtue so as to gain awareness of the whole. To develop "holiness within" was to yield "selfless action without." He experienced a *metamorphosis*, from anxiety to peace, from utter fear to reluctant acceptance, from the worry of mortality to an expectation that he would one day enjoy "the city of God."[6]

There are many examples in human history of a metamorphosis that occurs when a human experiences the divine. Often these experiences occur during moments of trauma, during mental or physical anguish, when healing is needed, and a metamorphosis occurs in mind and body, and time is briefly interrupted by the coming of the divine into transient human affairs. One of the most famous metamorphoses recounted in ancient literature occurred on a mountain in the region of Galilee.

The peaks of grand summits have historically attracted adventurers, seekers, questioners, thinkers. Standing at great height, above the clouds, surveying the earth, questions are answered, and problems solved. There is a clarity in the thin air. Even if mountain summits are often shrouded in clouds, there is an unmistakable sense of truth where strong winds meet bare stone. The duration of time matters very little on the windy summit, where such vastness extends before one's view, overwhelming everyday experience. People have often found the timeless on mountain tops. The ancient Greek gods resided on Mt. Olympus. Other mountains were sacred to the gods of Greece and elsewhere: Mt. Nysa was sacred to Dionysus, the Greek god of wine; Mt. Kyllene was sacred to Hermes, the messenger god; Mount Ida in Crete was sacred to the thunderer Zeus; the Hindus and Buddhists found Mt. Meru sacred; Cedar Mountain was sacred to Ishtar, the Babylonian goddess of love. The thunder and lightning upon Mt. Sinai compelled Moses to ascend its slopes where he discovered his destiny. The deceiver failed in his attempt to beguile Jesus on a mountain top.

Matthew and Luke's story implies what other passages in the Gospels make clear: Jesus sought out the Galilean and Judaean mountains, where he often went to pray and think.

In the vague chronology of the New Testament, "about eight days" (Luke) or "six days" (Matthew and Mark) after Jesus proclaimed to his disciples what he told the deceiver, that it is no good to sacrifice truth for power and wealth, Jesus and his closest followers Peter and the Zebedee brothers, James and John, ascended a mountain in Galilee.[7] There, on the summit, Jesus was, in Matthew and Mark's words, *metamorphosed* before them. This word, based on the Greek *metamorphosis*, is usually translated, *transfigured*, hence the incident is known as the *transfiguration*. Matthew says Jesus's clothes became dazzling white, and his face shone like the sun. Whatever the source was for this incident, apparently based on the eyewitness of Peter, John, or James, as in so many of the accounts of Jesus's life, Matthew, Mark, and Luke provide similar stories told slightly differently. Mark relates that Jesus's clothes became whiter than any fuller on earth could make them, but he does not refer to his shining face. Luke does not use the word *metamorphosis*, rather he says simply that Jesus's appearance changed, and his "raiment" became "gleaming white." All three accounts agree that after Jesus changed, two figures appeared, which the disciples interpreted to be Moses and Elijah.

Matthew says that as Jesus conversed with the two prophets, Peter matter-of-factly wondered whether or not he should build three tents, or shelters, for them. Then a divine cloud descended upon the mountain, and the disciples heard a voice from the cloud say: "This is my son, the beloved, in whom I am well pleased; listen to him." The disciples were understandably terrified, and prostrated themselves before the holy experience. But when they opened their eyes, the cloud and prophets had departed, and there was only Jesus, who told them not to be afraid. Then they descended the mountain.

Luke has a slightly different version. He says that Moses and Elijah were discussing Jesus's upcoming "exodus" in Jerusalem. But the disciples were "burdened with sleep"; as they came to their senses, they saw the two prophets departing, and Peter, slightly out of his mind, suggested that he build three tents, perhaps so the two prophets would stay. The cloud then descended upon them, and the disciples were afraid, especially when they heard God's voice say: "This is my son, the chosen one, hear him." Then the cloud disappeared, and Jesus and his three disciples were alone.

Mark's account has subtle differences from Luke and Matthew: he does not refer to the sleepiness of the disciples, but does suggest that Peter was disoriented when he suggested erecting the tents. All three gospel accounts state that Jesus ordered the disciples not to mention the incident; Mark and Matthew have Jesus tell them to keep silent until after, in Mark's words, the *Son of Man* should rise from the dead, which confused the disciples even more.

The transfiguration appears to be instance where God identifies Jesus as His chosen one, His only Son; a similar occurrence was Jesus's baptism, when the Holy Spirit descended upon him as he emerged from the water. These are events so out of the ordinary, so marked by the divine entering human experience, as to be miraculous, when the timeless enters time, confusing the sequence of events, the normal temporal experience of seconds, minutes, hours, days. The lack of clarity of this supposed chronological event, the transfiguration, explains why Matthew, Mark, and Luke have slightly different versions. It is difficult to have uniformity in narratives of historical events when such events do not follow the typical rules of cause and effect. Luke has the disciples sleeping because they were experiencing a dreamlike world not subject to the typical rules of time, so sleep becomes the metaphor for dealing with this experience. Indeed Luke uses the Greek word, *hypnos*, to describe their slumber. Who knows how long they were there? Luke implies they spent the night, so perhaps they did erect tents. But the experience could have been much longer, or much shorter. Hypnotic slumber is not conducive to keeping track of time. A person does not change appearance according to the rules of time—but there could be a change in a dreamlike, timeless world. To be reborn or transfigured—*metamorphosed*, in Paul's words—is an experience that usually takes much time, and is not something that occurs in an instant. Jesus, in a brief amount of time (a day or so), goes through a change that could take a lifetime.

The fourth gospel, John, does not include an account of the transfiguration on the mountain, though John provides numerous other examples, exclusive to his gospel, of similar, transformative experiences. When Jesus has an interview with the Pharisee Nicodemus, telling him that a person must be "born from above" to experience God's kingdom, Nicodemus is understandably confused, when human experience has only one birth, which begins human chronology on earth. Jesus's response that one must be born of the spirit, or wind, the origins and direction of which are never certain, makes little sense according to the human experience of time, though fits more appropriately in the dreamlike world of the timeless, of which Nicodemus, unlike Jesus, had little experience. Nicodemus was not the only person perplexed by Jesus's message in John's and the other Gospels. The Samaritan woman at the well; the Pharisees and Sadducees; Pontius Pilate; Judas, Thomas, indeed all the disciples; the shepherds in the field; the Magi; Zechariah; even

Mary and Joseph, were confronted with the irrational, unexpected, uncomfortable ways of God.

Paul (Hebrew, *Saul*) of Tarsus, a contemporary of Jesus, was like many of his time very skeptical when he heard the accounts of a Galilean healer who was crucified and raised from the dead. Paul was son of a tent-maker and Roman citizen who lived in Tarsus, a cosmopolitan city in southeastern Anatolia (present Turkey). His father was sufficiently successful to allow Paul the benefit of a good education—he became of a master of the Torah, the Law. He was probably, at least for a time, a student in Jerusalem. One of his mentors was Gamaliel, a leader of the Jerusalem Sanhedrin. Like most Pharisees Paul was conservative, dogmatic, and inflexible. When he heard that followers of the crucified Jesus of Nazareth were still spreading his teachings, Paul did what he could to repulse this intellectual invasion. The *Acts of the Apostles* records an incident where the follower of Jesus, Stephen, was stoned by an angry mob of Jews; Paul was in the midst of the crowd, in tacit approval of the murder. Later, having heard of an enclave of Christians at Damascus, he obtained permission of the high priest, Caiaphas, to journey to Damascus to search them out and rid the city of this heresy. On the road to Damascus, however, all the guilt over the sins of the preceding years caught up with Paul; he was blinded by a dazzling light accompanied by a voice that demanded, "Saul, Saul, why do you persecute me?" Paul was brought to his knees by the risen Christ. The experience changed him forever. He went to Damascus not to persecute but to recover his sight and to learn what was His will. Paul became the most fervent and dedicated apostle of the *word*: he became the great teacher of the Gentiles, the non-Jews, bringing the teachings of Jesus to Greeks and Romans. He was, as he wrote in his *Epistle to the Romans*, chapter twelve, "metamorphosed by the renewing of" his mind.

12

METAMORPHOSIS

My name is Legion; for we are many...
If ancient Mediterranean writing, such as the New Testament, was never clear about *when*, never had accurate chronologies and dates to guide the reader concerned with sequence of events, there was on the other hand much information about *who* and *what*, a consequence of the concern of ancient biographers and historians with moral episodes. Even if there are no dates, and chronology and sequence of events are distorted, in the Gospels, there are a lot of wonderful stories, especially about the man from Galilee, who spent much time in the seaport town of Capernaum, situated on the northern shores of the Sea of Galilee. He had a reputation for wonderful healings, of the blind, of lepers, of people who were close to death. He was known to have cast out demons from many people. He was known as a miracle-worker, reputedly able to command the elements, even the waters of the lake, to obey him.

Such were the stories told of this man: While in Capernaum, Jesus went to the synagogue, as he had previously in Nazareth, and read the Scripture and taught with unexpected authority. A man entered the synagogue who was set apart from the others in his actions, demeanor, and habits. People considered him possessed by "unclean spirits," that is, demons. The man demanded of Jesus the reason for his presence, what he wanted of them—the demon possessed—and that he knew who he really was, the "holy one of God." Jesus demanded of the demon that he exit the man, which occurred, with the man, or the demon, screaming and shouting. The witnesses, who included at least Simon Peter, his brother Andrew, and the two Zebedee brothers, James and John, were understandably astonished. And word spread throughout Galilee of the person who could command demons.

Not surprisingly, crowds of people came from all over Capernaum to Peter's house, where Jesus stayed, demanding that their demons of mind and body be exorcized. Jesus healed Peter's mother-in-law of fever, and many others of their physical and spiritual illnesses. The demons left these people silently, such was his power over them. When the people had departed, he renewed himself by going into the desert; there he spent the night in meditation and prayer. The next morning crowds of people were searching for him, so he departed Capernaum and traveled to other places, teaching and healing. His actions were cathartic to many. He met a man on the road with a skin ailment, such as leprosy; Jesus cleansed the man with the touch of his hand. Although Jesus admonished the healed man to keep silent, the word went out that Jesus could heal even lepers. He could no longer enter any town unnoticed, so he kept to the surrounding hills and desert, where even there he could be found by the perseverant.

After a time he slipped back into Capernaum unnoticed, staying at his or another's home, when he was discovered again. Soon the home was filled with those earnestly entreating him to teach and heal them. A paralyzed man and his companions heard of his discovery and decided to go for healing. When they arrived at the home there was no place to enter, such was the crowd. The men carrying the stretcher contrived to climb to the roof, where they removed enough thatch or tiles as to lower the paralytic among the crowd, next to Jesus. Everyone inside, including Jesus, was impressed by their resourcefulness, and their faith. Jesus then spoke to the paralytic, forgiving his sins. Not only does Mark imply that illness was considered a consequence of sin, but that Jesus had the authority to forgive sins. Such a remark could only bring questioning among Jews—the Sadducees and Pharisees—who considered God alone the forgiver of sins. Jesus sensed such questioning in the crowd, and wishing to illustrate his words with an example, said to the assembled crowd, and the paralytic: "that you may know that the Son of man has authority on earth to forgive sins . . . I say to you, rise, take up your pallet, and go home." The paralytic accordingly rose to his feet, healed of his illness.

Meanwhile, stories of the infamous demon-possessed man of the Decapolis had spread throughout the regions surrounding the Sea of Galilee. The healer heard of this man, and though he sought to restrict his activities to the Jews, and was not wont to visit Gentile territory, he decided to journey across the lake from Capernaum to Decapolis, to a place of the dead haunted by Legion. The accounts of this incident are unclear as to where exactly Jesus and the Demoniac (Legion) met: somewhere on the eastern shores of the Sea of Galilee, in the upper eastern Jordan valley.

Jesus arrived at grazing land abandoned to the tombs of the dead and herds of pigs. Legion, hiding among the tombs, filthy, frightened, forlorn, saw a crowd of people approaching; one man in particular stood out. The healer. Fear descended upon Legion.

He feared that he might hurt or kill the healer. Or, he feared that the healer might release the demons of his mind, these infernal companions that filled his days—and then what would Legion become? What happens to a person dominated by fear who no longer fears? The prospect was terrifying. If Legion and the Fear, so long inseparable, became separated, what then? Would there be only emptiness, even nonexistence? Fear, for all of its evil, has this one benefit: it fills the mind, distracts a person from reality, provides the security of knowing what to expect—anxious foreboding—minute by minute.

Nevertheless, the Demoniac approached the healer, and bared himself, made himself naked before him, surrendered to him. The healer asked his name. The Demoniac could only respond with the name that filled him, that dominated his being: *Legion*.

The New Testament is filled with demonology. In this story, demons within the Demoniac immediately recognized Jesus, and Legion, having never met Jesus, identified Jesus by name and referred to him as Son of God Most High. The demons demanded to know what Jesus wanted of them and pleaded that he would not torment them. Jesus called for the "unclean spirit" to leave the man. The thousands of demons inhabiting Legion begged Jesus not to send them into the abyss, which in the *Book of Revelation* is the place where Satan, the Beast, and demons reside/are confined. Rather, they asked that he allow them into a herd of pigs grazing upon a mountain side that descended precipitously into the sea. Jesus accommodated their request, and the demons went from Legion into the herd of unclean animals, which caused a stampede over the cliff into the water, where the swine drowned.

The herdsmen who witnessed this ran to tell the people in the surrounding region; they came to see what happened, and found Legion now sitting, clothed and rational, at the feet of Jesus. The locals heard how the Demoniac had been cured, and being afraid, asked Jesus to leave. Preparing to embark on a boat to return to the western shores of the Sea of Galilee, the now-healed Legion requested to join Jesus, who dismissed him saying to stay in the Decapolis and tell people what had happened, how he had been cured through God's mercy. Legion accordingly went to proclaim his healing throughout the region.

What did the former Demoniac, Legion, tell people? His was an age long before our's of reason and science and our realization of the absurdity of the stories of demonology contained within the New Testament. The Synoptic Gospel writers (Matthew, Mark, Luke) provided numerous accounts of demonic possession; indeed, it is often implied that those who are ill are demonized, and Jesus healed through exorcism, releasing a person from supernatural demonic possession. In the Synoptic Gospels, Jesus is a healer-exorcist. Also in the Synoptics, Jesus gives his disciples the power to exorcise demons. In the Gospel of John, Satan, the "ruler of the world" is head of the world's demonic forces. Satan personifies evil, which if it is still under God's control, is significant in human affairs. But Jesus, heralding the kingdom of God, will defeat the prince of the world and his forces. Luke describes the eschatalogical mission of Jesus defeating evil and demonic power when Jesus says: "I saw Satan fall like lightning from heaven."

Was Legion the Demoniac truly possessed by demons? Are there such entities as demons who enter our minds and beings and control or try to control us? Is there a spiritual and/or supernatural evil that can possess humans, animals, other things? In other words, does Satan really exist? Did Jesus truly heal by exorcism? Does healing today involve exorcism—if not, should it? If the story is not about exorcism, and the Demoniac was mentally disturbed, what explains the reasons why he was healed so quickly?

What are the demons that make up the legion of fear today? Many people over the centuries have experienced something like what the Demoniac of Decapolis experienced. *Legion* has inhabited people time and again. Are a person's obsessive images about death and destruction, obsessions that drive a person to despair time and again, the thousands, the legion, of fantastic chimera that possess a person, any different from the Demoniac's legion?

The demon in the story of the Demoniac is time. The burden of time, though not an independent Satanic demon, can still appear as an unclean spirit, can still be attached to the temptations of the deceiver, can still cause humans to flee from civilized society to haunt the tombs of the past. Time oppresses with legions of images of fear and failure, with an overwhelming collection of memories the weight of which burdens the present and makes the future intolerable to conceive. Whatever had happened to the Demoniac had made him insane with guilt, grief, and fear. The legion of demons was, in short, the weight of sin upon the human mind and soul, coloring Legion's beliefs, making him fear the present and the future, confusing him as to what was right and true and who he really was.

13

THE HEALER

The hem of his garment...

At the time in which Legion lived, the sickness of humankind was great. Illness pervaded mind and body, individually and collectively. There were many at the time who professed that they knew the art of healing, but there was only one healer. One might prescribe a purgative to cleanse the system; nevertheless, the evil remained. Another might advise cold baths and plenty of water; yet the filth could not be washed away. There were countless potions, some herbal some magical, but they had little but a brief calming or mystical effect that lasted only a short time, then the symptoms returned. The symptoms of the sick were widespread and common. It was a pandemic of chaos and hate. People acted in public one way and in private another, hiding the wretchedness of self. Sunny faces could hardly hide the darkness within. The mind might appear calm in the moment though the storms of the past and the high winds and seas of the future distracted and haunted. The present was never at peace where memory clouded the mind and anticipation loomed, a dark shadow of despair.

The mass of people lived in anticipation of something wonderful, something or someone who would save them from despair, loneliness, uncertainty, dread, and the relentless movement of time. A savior was needed. The previous centuries of thought and culture, politics and war, had taught the people that humans are not sufficient unto themselves, that alone they will ignore what is right and harmonious and destroy peace and truth.

All humans need healing. A woman in a crowd in first century Capernaum needed healing. She suffered from unremitting bleeding. According to the *Gospel of Mark*, she had tried the remedies of physicians, impoverishing herself in the process. Word of the healing of the Demoniac had anticipated Jesus's return from the region of Decapolis; a great crowd surrounded him; an important man, a local leader named Jairus, had approached Jesus in anguish over his desperately ill daughter. As Jesus and the crowd hurried to Jairus's home, the unnamed woman in the crowd reached out to touch the hem of Jesus's garment, telling herself that touching any part of so great a healer would cure her bleeding. Indeed, upon touching his garment the bleeding stopped; she felt herself immediately cured. Jesus, though surrounded by an eager crowd of people, felt some power (Greek *dynamin*) leave his body for another. He asked, "Who touched me?" The woman came forward and told her story of chronic illness and healing. Jesus told her, "your faith has made you well."

The greatest man in world history is a healer. His greatest attribute is love. He lives for others not himself. He brings not the promise of riches, glory, conquests, but peace, contentment, love. All that he teaches is unexpected. His words and actions contradict reason and experience. His actions are contrary to expectations. He says what is hurtful to the passive mind. He confuses the self-satisfied, and challenges the accepted viewpoint. He makes the forces of the moment, the authorities of the present, squirm uncomfortably in their recognition of his truth and their error. Under his tutelage and presence the false becomes true, the sick become well, the low become high, rigidity becomes fluidity, and what is normal vanishes in the wake of the uninvited. Illusions shatter. He makes the supernatural natural, the impossible possible, the unbelievable believable. His teachings challenge the truth of existence, the standards of society, the laws upon which humans live, preconceived notions, scientific evidence, and the objective mentality of logic and reason.

The *sine qua non* of his healing, teaching, understanding, and intuition—that inner sight, that penetration into others—is empathy. His is a fundamental, a pure empathy, one described inadequately by words that produce images and concepts readily identified by the mind. His empathy is that of the quick glance that produces the long gaze into the soul; the touch of the hand that brings knowing peace to the recipient; the word that expresses what is most longed for; the thought that is not fleeting, of the immediate moment, but all-encompassing, mirroring one's very being. What are to most mere fleeting moments of empathetic awareness is to him universal, without exception.

He heals the great of their arrogance, and brings them low; the weak of their loneliness and insecurity, wraps them in love; the violent of their aggression, torturing them with guilt and regret; the sick with hope; the homeless with a wonderful place in the soul; the vanquished with the future promise of victory; victors of their hubris; those tortured by anxiety with peace of mind; hate with love; the anguished past with the contented present; the earth its scars with beautiful life and growth; the disease of being unwanted, the disease of no hope, no cure; death with life. He heals all.

The Greek word for healing used in the New Testament, *therapeu*, literally means to relieve disease—disease is never vanquished, nor the body's tendency toward illness replaced with complete health; rather, disease is relieved, but temporarily —Jesus does not cure people from physical decay and death.

What is healing but a search to find health and completeness; to stave off for a time death and pain; to break from the binds of illness; to feel free even when the imprisonment of illness will one day take hold; to feel eternity if for a moment; happiness before the alternative sets in; strong even if weakness follows; content even when discontent is around the corner? One knows that age, the longer one lives, will bring increased suffering and pain, something of a sense of slow death—or as Michel de Montaigne said, each day we die a bit more. The youth seeks adulthood; the adult seeks youth again—but time forbids the return.

A truth of healing is this: healing of the body is short term, for death will occur; physical healing is temporary and transient. Healing of the mind is also limited, for with increased age the mind will decay as well, though at different rates from the body. The mind will always be tugged in different directions by memory, present awareness, and expectation of what is to come. Time forces upon the mind the tempestuous combination of guilt and recollection of pleasure, current transient pleasure or pain, and foreboding and fear of what will be. Can the mind, experiencing only the present, be made whole when each moment is just a brief part? Doubtful. The only true healing, then, is of the *soul* or the *self* or the *being*, that which is the ego, the *I*, which forms the sum of each person, which transcends one's own experience of time, which transcends time itself. The *soul, self, being* is comprised of the body and mind, yet it is something more, something difficult to define, difficult to know. But it can be sensed, it is present if only in a vague, amorphous way. Maybe the best definition for it is "I am," which Jesus proclaimed to the Jews, as recorded in the *Gospel of John*. He knew what the *soul, self, being* is, and he proclaimed it confidently. The Gospel is a proclamation of what the *soul, self, being* is, and how healing from the limitations of the past, present, and future occurs. The writer of the *Gospel of John* must have experienced this awareness, and seeking to define what Jesus was and what he meant by "I am," declared him the *logos*, the thought and word that transcends time, which was the clearest expression of the "I am" proclamation, the *soul, self, being*, that existed in the first century, *Anno Domini*. The attempt to know and understand the *soul, self, being* is the basis for all the world's religions and the great philosophies of all times and places. It is in Buddhism as the ultimate breaking from the self, Taoism as the *way* away from the self, Neoplatonism as that which encompasses all selves, Transcendentalism as a world or universal Self that we all partake in.

All of these religions and philosophies have a sense of ultimate irony, that the individual self experiencing time seems to restrict us from the *soul, self, being*; that through each self we know the *soul, self, being* and want to attain it but find the self restrictive. The individual self of a specific time and place allows us a glimpse into the true *soul, self, being* of all times and places, yet we glimpse as well that the former is not the latter, and indeed the former only allows us to glimpse, allows us a hint of, the latter: but how one leads to the other is an uncertain path. Some would say there is no path from one to the other; others would say that there is a path, but it is narrow indeed; others would say that the path is for all people, but it must await death; others, that it can be found in this life, but through tremendous denial of the urges of self.

Jesus proclaimed that it is through him that each person can come to know the *soul, self, being,* that he encompasses that hidden thing within us that is never explicitly known, that to know Him is to know the *soul, self, being,* that to know the *soul, self, being,* to accept its presence, is to be healed of the dictatorship of time and the death of body and mind. Jesus's own body and blood, his own suffering and fear, his own struggle in time, his own torturous death, represent the liberation of the whole of humanity, each person, from time and the sickness of body and mind. The liberation is an acceptance of what is, what transcends time, what exists within each of us, the *soul, self, being,* that is resurrected upon death, or rather freed by death, freed from time and ignorance, and the *soul, self, being* exists again but in a transcendent form, not bound by time, but transcending time. The ascent to Heaven is the ascent from time and space of the *soul, self, being* into something, some form of existence that is not understandable to those still limited by time. Jesus is the one to have completely understood it, he is the path to it, he is the *Son of Man* in that he is the way, truth, and life for all who seek to know what this *soul, self, being* is.

The woman of Capernaum with the hemorrhage experienced momentary healing and the vision of the *soul, self, being* when power went from Jesus into her. What was this power, and how did it heal?

The power is the intuitive recognition of love. It enabled the woman to have the awareness of God's grace. The power is an enabling, a growing awareness of God, to know He exists and cares, that He is embracing us so that we will conform to His will, His grace, in our thoughts and actions. People healed by Jesus experience not only physical healing but the power of God's grace and love as well. The *dynamos*, the power or virtue described by Luke, is the power over death, the virtue of life.

14

THE TEACHER

B*lessed are...*
When and what sort of day it was is unknown, though probably it was in the dry, summer months when the breezes come off the Sea of Galilee and temper the sweltering heat of the noonday sun. Nor is it known where it occurred—the writer of the *Gospel of Matthew* claims that Jesus of Nazareth stood atop a hill to address the people surrounding him, seeking healing and redemption. The author of the *Gospel of Luke*, the only other written account of the "sermon on the mount," suggests that it did not occur on a hill at all, rather on a broad plain. Matthew places the sermon at some point early in Jesus's ministry, shortly after his baptism by John the Baptist and his call of the first disciples. Luke puts it later in time, but like Matthew, after Jesus has healed many people, which explains the crowds. Luke says the sermon occurred after several situations in which the Pharisees and Sadducees challenged Jesus's authority. One of these challenges, when Jesus's disciples picked and ate kernels of wheat on the Sabbath, suggests that if the sermon took place

soon after, as implied in Luke's gospel, then it was during late summer or early autumn. The two gospel writers agree on the large numbers of people that arrived to hear Jesus, to touch him, to be healed by him. His reputation as a healer had spread throughout Judaea, including Jerusalem, north into Galilee and the towns of the Decapolis, and northwest to Syria, even to the Phoenician towns of Tyre and Sidon.

Notwithstanding the impatience of the crowd, Jesus taught them before he healed them. Yet his lesson that day had everything to do with healing. He told them of life and its uncertain meaning, of behavior and the confusing nature of what is right and wrong, of the misperception of the importance of wealth and the greatness of the powerful. Some of his teachings seemed understandable, as they were based on the Law of Moses and Psalms of David. If you think you know the meaning of the Law and the poetry of David, he said, you do not. The Law of Moses was for an obstinate people who had little faith and more doubt. The Psalms reflected the thinking of a warlord and man of violence who had discovered a higher saving power and was willing to put his trust in Him. So much of what Jesus said contradicted the experience of the everyday. How can the poor be blessed when they are spat upon, ignored, hungry, sick, and cold? In the world of Rome, the meek were enslaved, and yet Jesus said the blessed include those who are afraid, who give in, who surrender, who are injured, raped, imprisoned, murdered, and made homeless strangers. How will the hungry be filled? Who will dry the tears of those who weep? And when are the merciful rewarded? Not in this world, not in this time. His listeners were confused: how could they not be? But if the mind, thoughts in this one moment of time, could not follow his teachings, the feelings and tacit understanding of the emotions knew that this was the Truth. There was liberation in what he said. There was the path to happiness in his words. There was satisfaction with self, meaning in life, contentment with experience no matter what life brings, and wisdom that comes from accepting the will of God.

Matthew and Luke agree on the general scope of the Beatitudes, though they differ on some particulars. Matthew, for example, records Jesus as having initiated the sermon with the comment, "Blessed are the poor in spirit, for of them is the kingdom of the heavens." Luke records a more terse, less confusing comment, stating simply, "Blessed are the poor, because yours is the kingdom of God." Whereas Luke then records Jesus as saying, "Blessed are the ones hungering now, for you will be satisfied," Matthew records a comment of more depth: "Blessed are those hungering and thirsting for righteousness, for they shall be satisfied." Luke has Jesus say, "Blessed are those weeping now, for they shall laugh," while Matthew's gospel says, "Blessed are the mourning, for they shall be comforted." Matthew continues: "Blessed are the meek, for they shall inherit the earth. . . . Blessed are the merciful, for they shall obtain mercy. Blessed are the clean in heart, for they shall see God. Blessed are the peacemakers, for they shall be called sons of God. Blessed are those being persecuted for the sake of righteousness, for of them is the kingdom of the heavens." All of these are omitted by Luke. Only the last of Matthew's beatitudes is echoed by Luke: "Blessed are you when they reproach you and persecute and say all evil against you lying for the sake of me." The many didactic comments that follow the Beatitudes are much more numerous in Matthew than in Luke, who differs also from Matthew in his statements of woe to the wealthy, the full, the happy, and the self-satisfied.

The blessed man is a teacher. He imparts his intuitive knowledge by means of stories and poetic verse. People come from far and wide to hear him because he teaches with authority, imparted to him from personal challenge and lonely reflection. He teaches with gentle words that question cherished ideals and challenge fundamental assumptions. His words shock and console at the same time. He teaches of a love never known as love, of courage that appears cowardly, of obedience to those whom one most wants to disobey. His teachings reject the goals of one's life, one's ambitions of success, the accepted means to achieve personal happiness, the bases of human relations. He leaves his listeners inspired, chagrined; excited, exhausted; joyous, in tears; hopeful, without hope. Such is the shattering impact of sight upon blindness, light upon darkness, truth upon error.

Many of his listeners had the same demonic fears as Legion. The current Hellenistic teachings hardly brought consolation, rather pain. The stories and lessons of the Hebrew Bible terrified people with legendary and historical tales of God's wrath. The myths, philosophy, and religious offerings of the Graeco-Roman world offered nothing better, rather dark, depressing stories of fate and the demise of heroes. A different teaching was needed.

The teachings of Jesus of Nazareth defy codification, ritualization, elevation to a *Rule, Commandment,* a standard for all human behavior. This is his genius: he speaks to each person notwithstanding the gulf of time, experience, or personality. Each one hears him differently. His teaching is not a formula to be memorized but a word of subtle, invisible transformation. Those who know should not listen; his word is meant for those who seek a personal truth rather than a creed or dogma. He addresses great crowds of hearers each of whom considers himself a pupil quite alone with the teacher.

Such was the message of the *Parable of the Sower,* one of his many stories, homely examples from daily existence, that address the whole of life.

A sower went out to sow. And as he sowed, some seed fell along the path, and the birds came and devoured it. Other seed fell on rocky ground, where it had not much soil, and immediately it sprang up, since it had no depth of soil; and when the sun rose it was scorched, and since it had no root it withered away. Other seed fell among thorns and the thorns grew up and choked it, and it yielded no grain. And other seeds fell into good soil and brought forth grain, growing up and increasing and yielding thirtyfold and sixtyfold and a hundredfold.

The sower of seed is a metaphor for society, culture, life itself. Some seeds that are planted, some lives started, some projects begun, some thoughts thought, never take root, but are quickly extinguished, destroyed. Other lives, thoughts, actions, projects begin but are never fully embraced, never fully engaged in, accepted, or take root, and they quickly wither and die or are abandoned. Other lives, thoughts, actions, projects take root but their energy is quickly spent, the enthusiasm quickly diminished, often in the face of illness, adversity, threats, or temptations, and they die and fail as well. But some lives, thoughts, actions, projects are healthy, well thought out, pursued, and take root to flourish and succeed.

Common sense allows for quick and easy interpretation of the parables; the parables express truths found in everyday life. But Jesus had a deeper, hidden meaning in his parables. The true meaning of the parable of the sower, he told his disciples, is: The sower is Jesus who sows the *word* of God. Some people hear the word but it makes no impact and they remain in Satan's hands, remain devoted to sin. Some hear the word and quickly seize upon it but it does not last, sin quickly takes over, and they remain unredeemed. Others hear the word and embrace it, begin to live their lives by it, but some other attraction, temptation, concern, challenge distracts them from the word, and they return to the unredeemed life of sin as well. But some hear the word, are changed by it, live their lives by it, and they are fully redeemed, live a life of plenty in the knowledge of the word.

Interestingly, Jesus told his disciples that his interpretation, the true way of understanding the parable, is reserved only for his close followers. Those who are ignorant of his teaching will remain ignorant. Those who embrace his teaching will be allowed full access to the meaning of the *word*. But does this not contradict another of his teachings about how those who have not will have, those who are low will become high? Why would he not want all people to know the true meaning of his words? Why would he want to restrict his teaching to a small and exclusive group of followers?

The *word* cannot be understood quickly and easily, is not something to be bandied about as a commodity. The *word* must be treasured, and those who are meek and poor in spirit, the humble and those yearning for truth and peace, are the ones who deserve this teaching. Those who *already know*, such as the Pharisees and Sadducees, do not deserve this teaching, which is reserved for those who do not know. The Pharisees do not have the hearts and minds prepared for a different kind of teaching; they arrogantly assume they know the truth, which condemns them.

The rich soil, therefore, that can receive the seed of the *word* is the soil of a mind open to God, open to different possibilities, not preset, predetermined, already clear and knowing of the truth. The danger is that one will become a *pharisee* without even knowing it, that one will come to believe that *he knows*, and there can be no other truth than his own. Only God knows. A person must never lose the innocence of seeking to know, of having the humility or poverty of spirit to remain open to what God can teach.

For what does one live? For wealth, power, beauty, duration of life, luxury, pleasure, honor, glory? What are all of these but fleeting temptations in contradiction to transcendent truths? What good is wealth if truth, love, beauty, life cannot be bought? Upon what thrones do dead kings sit? What ruler who enjoys absolute power knows peace and contentment, who does not lie awake at night listening to every terrifying sound of impending doom, hidden assassins, violent rebellion? How many words of truth does the leader hear from the obsequious, the panderer, the false friend? How often is power stable, resting content, secure, rather than at odds, in defense, threatened? Likewise beauty is always on the run from age and ugliness; the mirror which when young is a constant companion and friend is when old the feared and distant enemy. How shallow indeed is one's existence if the title, the award, notoriety, and fame fill one's short life. Who shall remember tomorrow's dust? If one's friends are the adoring unknown of future ages then one is lonely indeed. The fleeting, the transparent, the transient, are the stuff of fear.

What appears real is not: the apparent strong are weak; the great are without significance; the purported wise are filled with ignorance. The poor, however, will someday be rich; the humble will be glorified; the weak will in time have a kingdom. He who resists the temptations of love will know love everlasting. He who fights will never find peace. Allow the strong and violent your wealth, your property, your life. When they die you will yet live. When someone does you wrong, bless them. What good is it to condemn and to resist? All the wrongs, and slights, and sins of others against you are incomparable to those seen in the mirror. *Go, and sin no more.*

He teaches love. This is the greatest truth, from which all else flows. Love is a result of reflection. One cannot love in a vacuum of personal and spiritual knowledge. Look within to see who one truly is, simply human. Give in to oneself, break down internal barriers. Trust in oneself. Trust one's feelings. Seek the core of being, the truth, the touch of the divine upon one's soul. Know love within, then unleash the torrent that flows from one to another, one's neighbor, all men and women. Look without fear into the eyes of another. See the divine within another, a mirror reflection of oneself, a mirror unto God. See within not the contradictory, the violent, the ugly, the fearful, but the beauty and love of God.

He teaches the knowledge and love of God by subtle self-reflection. One feels the overwhelming truth, the all-encompassing reality, the sum of being, in the unexpected, normal, perfunctory of existence. God is less apt to be found in a cathedral than in a forest the silence of which overwhelms save for the trickling brook and the gentle zephyr flowing through leaves and branches. Even amid the minutiae of time, the passing of one event upon another, stands the sameness of creation, the recurrent in feeling and life, the redundancy of nature. Time, the apparent antithesis of God, is ironically the precise means by which to discover His presence.

Everything has a past, seen at the moment of looking upon another human, oneself, or a natural phenomenon. Time culminates in the constantly refreshed and renewed present. At each moment one inquires into oneself, to know the sum of past moments, to reconcile time, self, with the timeless, God. At each moment one balances the present with the past: is what has been done, what is being done, right? Of the countless alternatives that have been chosen, will the choice be correct? Choice is made according to ignorance, an unknown future. Has the future becoming the present becoming the past confirmed or denied goodness?

He teaches that life is filled not with contingencies, rather possibilities. Love slowly unravels a philosophical knot. If God wills all things how can humans exercise free will? If humans exercise free will what role then has a providential God? Can God know all things, such as the future, yet not exercise His will? Is knowledge tied to action, determined by foresight? Dichotomies mix up thinking, to be sure. Human knowledge, will, and power appear in direct contrast to God's knowledge, will, and power. Otherwise humans would be on the same plane as God; but a vast gulf of time and eternity, human frailty and divine power, obviously exists. But God is not subject to human imagination and reason, which attempts to vainly divide God and humans more for the latter's rather than the former's glory. God's will is wrapped up in oneself—now, a minute ago, a minute to come. One's will is wrapped up in God's—now, a minute ago, a minute to come. Reason, actions, logic, observations, cannot teach us this truth. The teacher knows. Divine and human will unite in love as well as in all other intuitive, transcendent feelings of empathy, closeness, peace, tranquility, regret, expectation, yearning, homesickness, loneliness, warmth—all feelings of a moment that transcend the moment. Love reveals the simple yet profound dictates of one's own will and God's will.

Everyone that loveth is born of God, and knoweth God.

No one *knows* God, nor has He ever been seen. Yet those who love know God, have seen God, in their daily lives, in the eyes of another, in the cries of the child, in the consolation of the hurt, in the tears over the dead. God reveals Himself only through Love—it is *Elder Scripture.*

He teaches acceptance of the past—in so doing one transcends the past, comes to *be*, to know what *is*. All human history culminates in each moment, in each person. To accept oneself is to accept all humankind notwithstanding the diverse beliefs, customs, institutions, languages, and habits that comprise world peoples. One must accept sin, ignorance, evil. To accept is to halt resistance, to stop replaying it in one's mind, to quit making human actions the point of it all, and to simply be. To experience being in the singular moment is to transcend the burden of the past and the future. One therefore, in accepting time, accepts as well the transcendent, which one continually denies even as one feels it. It is easy to resist the transcendent and to put the blame on evil, or society, or the environment, or the past, or another. To accept the transcendent is to surpass sin, human limitations, evil, fear, the past, and the future.

The teacher knows from personal experience, having himself confronted, struggled with, and accepted his past—in so doing he released himself from fear and uncertainty. Jesus's teaching on time is revealed by one of his closest disciples, John son of Zebedee. In the *Gospel of John*, Jesus is the eternal word, the *logos*, not born in the traditional sense of created by God in the act of conception in the woman's womb, rather he is co-eternal, *is*, God become incarnate. The typical sense of the human experience of time—birth, life, death—is disrupted by the incarnate God coming into the world. John implies the confusion that results when he says, in chapter one, that John the Baptist precedes Christ's coming, but in reality, as the Baptist tells others, although it will appear that Jesus comes after him in reality he comes before him, existing first. The order and sense of time are confused by Christ's coming: the *logos* is already in time; we are just now made aware of it. This confusion is made apparent at the wedding at Cana, where Jesus turns the water into wine; the master of the feast notes that it is best, and typically is reserved till later in the feast. The traditional sequence of events, therefore, has been altered by Jesus. In the first few chapters John refers to "the first day," "the second day," implying chronological order, which is made nonsensical by the episodic nature of the retelling of events during Jesus's time on earth. The Jews, with a traditional sense of time's order, are put into a conundrum by Jesus's interpretation of time. When in John, 2:19, Jesus tells the Jews, "destroy this temple and in three day's I will raise it up," they assume that Jesus is talking about a building and a traditional sense of time—the temple took forty-six years to build! But Jesus is referring to the temple of his body, which reveals how his interpretation of time is personal, based on his own bodily sense of time, rather than public, based on the people's sense of time.

Jesus's unique interpretation of time is illustrated again in John, chapter three, when he converses with the Pharisee Nicodemus. Jesus uses veiled and strange words to indicate his sense of salvation, which is dependent neither upon time nor place; it is like the wind. Jesus confuses Nicodemus when he says that one must be "born again," a reference to a person experiencing a new beginning, not in time, through movement and growth, but in beliefs and personality, in the core of being not subject to time. Jesus tells Nicodemus that a person does not know where the spirit comes from or where it goes, that is, the past and the future, but only that it is, in the present. Those born of the spirit, born again, do not know the origins of the spirit of revelation, of their destiny.

In chapter four, John provides the example of the Samaritan woman and Jacob's well, which again reveals Jesus's unique sense of personal time. In the story, Jesus arrives at a particular time and place; it is the sixth hour. A woman arrives (by apparent happenstance) to draw water. Jesus requests a drink of real water in time to quench his bodily thirst acquired during travel. In response to her confusion (that a Jew would request a drink from a Samaritan), he says that he can provide her with a drink of water that transcends time; this drink quenches thirst, period. By quenching thirst, this drink stops thirst, bodily movement that brings about thirst, stops time, hence no more bodily thirst in time. In this singular moment, the transcendence is gained, life that lasts an eternity, everlasting, that is, a singular moment than continues on and on. Jesus then tells the woman that there will come a time, and the time is now, in the present, when worshipers will not worship at a place, but in spirit and truth, that is, not according to time and space, but in the singular moment. For something to be coming but is, becoming and being, shows again that in the presence of the *logos*, time is altered. The woman then says the messiah is coming; Jesus contrasts this future-oriented statement with the proclamation, "I am," meaning that the messiah is now, in the moment, and not in the future. When she leaves the disciples ask Jesus to eat, but he refuses this momentary bodily nourishment, claiming that he has food that is spiritual, that transcends the moment. Emphasizing this, he mentions the saying, four months then the harvest; he says on the contrary that the harvest is already present. The traditional sense of time, moment by moment, is distorted in this episode, and indeed, in many other episodes that follow in John's Gospel.

Jesus's philosophy of personal time, revealed in the Gospel of John, appears to have been the approach of Mary the mother of Jesus to reflecting on her son's life. Twice in the *Gospel of Luke* (2: 19 and 2: 51), Mary responded to the amazing events she had experienced and witnessed—the virgin birth, shepherds proclaiming the Messiah, prophecies of Simeon and Anna, and Jesus's statement in the temple that "I must be in my father's house"—not logically or rationally, which was impossible, rather intuitively, pondering such events in her heart. Following Mary, the person seeking to understand the life of Jesus must use personal time, pondering in one's heart the events recorded in the four Gospels.

Jesus's unique sense of time enabled him to teach his followers with confidence that "I am," having transcended the limitations of the past and the burden of the future. He has become content in the singular moment. He sees himself as human, as representing all humans, as present in all humans in a wonderful, mysterious way. He is the essence of humanity we see in another's eyes. His image is stamped on all humans, hence all humans are equal and good, to be cherished not destroyed, forgiven not condemned, helped to life not discontinued in life. His is the will active and present at all times. His is the love inherent in all acts.

> For through him all things came to be.

These words come from the *Gospel of John*, which is fourth in rank but also according to modern scholars fourth in time, being the last Gospel written, and fourth in accuracy and importance. John's Gospel is unique in that it seems less biographical, more mystical—hence modern skeptics conclude that it is not a valid source for the life of Jesus, though it is a valid source for the beliefs of early Christians. Yet if the Gospels of Mark, Luke, and Matthew are more down to earth and comparable to each other, hence according to the standards of internal source criticism easier to verify, it is John that speaks not so much to the mind as to the heart. If the synoptic Gospels seem more accurate, John's Gospel seems more *true*.

Jesus teaches of himself. According to the *Gospel of John*, chapter eight, Jesus proclaimed to the Pharisees of Jerusalem, "Truly, truly, I say to you, before Abraham was, I am." Could any two words be more significant, more compelling, that "I am"? In these two words I see that *I am*, that the Son of Man is in me, that the Son of Man is the symbol for me, a human. The theme of the Gospel is that Jesus is the *word*, the *logos*, the timeless entity, the source of being—an idea well known to the Greeks.

According to John, Jesus was all these things—and more. Jesus was not a disembodied idea, a mere thought, a *word* spoken then forgotten. "The word became flesh." An eternal, transcendent idea, a being of timeless thought and power, a singular moment, became something corporeal, merged with time, lived and died. The transcendent became transient; the eternal moment became a succession of moments.

Jesus teaches of the kingdom: not the kingdom that humans expect, the kingdom of power and wealth that will reign over all the world's peoples in coming centuries. Nor is his image of a king a titled prince of glory and riches, who wields his scepter over all the world. His is a kingdom of humble acts, of simple pleasures, of empathy and love, of complete and utter forgiveness of others for errors and transgressions, of embracing all peoples and loving them as oneself. His is a kingdom that exists forever in the single moment, a kingdom that ignores past and future for the present, a kingdom of the transcendent, that simply is, now, in you, in me, in all of us. He teaches of an existential kingdom of God.

Jesus teaches faith. From such a foundation one is armed against life's contingencies. Faith softens the blows of time. Faith opens up a world of understanding, and one sees continuity rather than fragments, unity rather than discord. Faith helps one conquer the immense possibilities opened up by the imagination. The temptation of greatness, of power, of fame and wealth, yield to simple acceptance of oneself. Deep within emerges a swell of insight and certainty. Time, the great tempter, yields to faith, the great healer.

Faith overwhelms the passing moments, and one learns not to bend, to doubt, to give in to the imaginary fears that feast upon the banquet of never-ending minutes and hours, a rich temporal food for the glutton of disbelief. Faith is unlearned, a product not of reason, nor of its agent time. Rather faith comes to the one who seizes upon God's will, who opens oneself, completely accepts God's benevolence, who asks blindly in prayer for unknown grace, but who asks all the same, and receives a hidden answer of subtle confidence in things as they are and things as they will be.

Jesus teaches acceptance. Jesus probed deep within the human psyche to see that humans profess but do not feel so important, strong, wealthy, and powerful, because there is always present the fear of riches, power, beauty, and youth being taken away. Life is about acceptance, not resistance. Accept, he told his listeners, your lot, your poverty, your weakness, your ignorance, your nakedness, the thorns of your flesh, your ugliness, your obesity, your fears, your mortality, the fleetingness of life, the movement of time, which ends in death. Accept the pattern of life, what is right and necessary. Surrender; make the choice not to choose; and the waters of necessity will baptize with love.

Accept the present, which is the means by which to know, simply, life. Life is a presence in the singular moment; it compels; it terrifies. Life in the present moment is something to treasure, to worship, as divine.

All of these teachings as relayed and hinted at in the Gospels, some of which Jesus told his followers on set occasions, such as during the Sermon on the Mount, were doubtless imparted to Legion in those moments—seconds, minutes, hours, days?—in which he met with Jesus, and was healed.

15

SON OF MAN

The Son of Man must suffer many things...
The mirror of the past is the only way to peer at the image of the Son of Man. The reflection is darkened by time and sin. Specters of the dead, haunting the dusty stacks of long-ago thoughts, turn up repeatedly, if indistinctly, on library shelves and in the dens of archivists. Storytellers such as the Greek Homer, abstract philosophers such as the Athenian Plato and John the Evangelist, poets such as King David and the Italian Petrarch, historians such as the Romans Livy and Tacitus, biographers such as the Greek Plutarch and the Physician Luke, essayists such as the Roman Seneca, the emperor Marcus Aurelius, and the Frenchman Michel de Montaigne, lived the past, made it their own, spoke to it and heard a response. Such writers expressed empathy toward past lives that span the ages. They engaged in a dialogue with the past, a discussion of self in light of others, creating a sensitive portrait, based on the varied experiences of humans at particular places and times, of the image of God in man, the Son of Man, apparent throughout the ages. This is true history.

Of the many forms of identification of Jesus of Nazareth used by himself and others—Messiah, Christ, Son of God, Logos, Word, *I am*, Lamb of God, Good Shepherd, Savior, Bread of Life, The Way—the identify he used most often, according to the Gospel writers, was *Son of Man*. Jesus's use of the phrase is as mysterious today as it was two thousand years ago. What he meant by Son of Man has confused his followers both then and now. And yet it is in his adopted title, his chosen identity, that we see clearly what *Anno Domini*, "in the year of our Lord," truly means, and why measuring our lives according to Christ's coming continues to be a useful device to understand our existence, human existence, in light of the existence of the anointed one, the Son of Man.

The phrase *Son of Man* appears repeatedly in the Old Testament and in other contemporary Hebrew and Greek writings. The notion of a "primordial" human was well known to the Greeks, who among the many choices from their heroic literature saw in the titan Prometheus the archetype of humankind. In the *Book of Genesis*, Adam brought suffering upon himself and his descendants because of his will and curiosity. Each human is a son of Adam (literally, son of *man*) in the ongoing search to exert one's own thought and will upon the future—this is the core of the idea of original sin. Gnostic Christians in the centuries after the death of Jesus identified Jesus with what they called the *anthropos*, "the primal father of the whole, the primal beginning, and the primal incomprehensible,"[1] which echoed the opening lines of the *Gospel of John*: "In the beginning was the word, and the word was with God, and the word was God."

God the *anthropos* was the being from whose image *man* derived. The Son of Man was the son of *anthropos*, the archetypal human, the son of God. The idea that Jesus was a *man* (Hebrew *adam*, Aramaic *nasha*, Greek *anthropos*) is accepted matter-of-factly in the New Testament. The Apostle Paul developed a powerful theology built upon the assumption that Jesus could die for human sin simply because as a man (*anthropos*) he experienced time, ignorance, pain, and, indirectly, sin. Indeed, some Biblical scholars argue that *son of man* was a phrase put into the mouth of Jesus by early Christians later in the first century, *Anno Domini*, so to fulfill their own expectations.

Jesus's disciples, according to the Gospels, were repeatedly mystified by how his actions and teachings contradicted the identity of *son of man* derived from Hebrew writers. Daniel in the Old Testament expected a Messianic Son of Man, to whom "was given dominion and glory and kingdom, that all peoples, nations, and languages should serve him," a "dominion" that is "everlasting" and which will neither "pass away" nor "be destroyed." During the first century, *Ante Christos*, the Hebrew writer Enoch predicted "a divine pre-existent figure," a Son of Man who was a destroyer of the enemies of the Jews.[2] The Jews of Jesus's time waited for a Son of Man along the lines of Daniel or Enoch rather than a Son of Man who was a humble carpenter, who practiced nonresistance and humility, who was willing to put love before the Judaic Law, who consorted with prostitutes rather than princes, paupers rather than Pharisees, who performed the most menial tasks, such as washing his disciples's feet, and who allowed himself to be taunted and tortured, scourged and crucified, as if he were a common thief. Jesus's disciples, confused by his death, had been so devoted to the traditional interpretation of the Son of Man as to fail to perceive his true significance until after the resurrection.

The Jews believed the Son of Man would be a distinct and unique individual, a kingly, even celestial, figure of a particular time and place. But Jesus claimed himself a human of no particular time or place. In the *Gospel of John* Jesus portrayed his time on earth as but a moment, like a single ray of light moving toward darkness: "Yet a little while is the light with you. Walk while ye have the light, lest darkness come upon you." Jesus's portrayal of himself created a metaphor for the individual's confrontation with a past burdened by doubt and uncertainty as well as an anticipated future that does not yet exist in time, yet exists in the mind, or being, of the individual. The Son of Man is God become man, which is to say He transcends time, the ongoing passage of events, by means of the singular moment where duration—time, past and future—has no meaning.

Jesus claimed he was the Son of Man who was introducing in the present moment of time the dawning Kingdom of God, now, in this instant, within each and every person. After telling the Samaritan woman who gave him a drink that the water he gives to people "will become . . . a spring of water welling up to eternal life," he told her that such a drink "now is." Once again these words found little acceptance in first century Palestine among those who sought, if anything, a future temporal Kingdom of God of wonder and power, or a future, heavenly, spiritual Kingdom of God akin to the Heavenly City of the Greek philosophers. But a Kingdom of God in the present moment of existence? How can this be? How can God's kingdom exist now rather than in the future?

The Son of Man bringing forth a Kingdom of God in the present moment: What could be more contradictory to the expectations of the first century as well as to our own time? It is easier to contemplate a perfect Messiah, a Lamb of God, who comes for a short visit to save the world, through whose resurrection the chosen will be saved, and in time enjoy eternal life. The implication of an *existential* Kingdom of God, however, is that the Son of Man is completely joined with, recreated in, time, present in each moment of existence, present in each one of us, each human, inextricably linked to human existence. How then can we know him? Through introspection, yes, and Scripture, too—but also through our own past experiences. For there is a reason why God chose to experience time. As Aurelius Augustine knew, each and every personal life experience yields knowledge of the Son of Man. Augustine wrote his autobiography, the *Confessions*, to explore this realization. To know this personal savior, this Son of Man as He has been manifested through human lives, including one's own, one must engage in the search for the Son of Man by means of a personal dialogue with the past, with Jesus' past, but more, with His life as it has been revealed through the lives and works of other humans. The presence of the Son of Man in all human lives is what Jesus meant when he declared, "I am." When Jesus died for our sins he died for human sin found in each and every historical event; he died for the personal and collective human past; he died for human history itself. Reflected in the mirror of time, the experience of the Son of Man reveals the truth of the past, present, and future: all people, all experiences, all humans, all love.

No one knows what the Son of Man looked like; no image of words or paint exists. To describe and to draw a collage of the varied experiences of humans over time is to create an accurate portrait of the Son of Man as a manifestation of the transcendent in human history.

We identify ourselves with others often through how we appear. We will like or be attracted, or hate or be repelled, by another's appearance, clothes, hair, face, color, etc. This limits us, however, as we often are seeking a mirror image. Jesus is appearance-less, purposely. We have no idea what his face was like, his hair, his skin color, his height, and weight. He could have been terribly ugly or short, or very tall or of average height. Perhaps he was disabled or physically impaired in some way. Jesus had an inner sight not relying on conventional sight; was he visually impaired? He healed the blind so many times. Was his healing based on his own experience? His healing, his teaching reaching to the core of humanity, was unencumbered by the distraction of sight. His strongest sense appeared to be touch rather than sight, hearing, taste, smell. His healing of the physically impaired could have derived from the experience of his own weakness, his own physical impairment, which he turned to power and strength. For the same reason that Jesus had to know human nature and sin to save us from sin, so he had to know physical, spiritual, even mental and emotional disability to heal similar illnesses and weaknesses

Strange that no one ever commented on how Jesus looked. No one ever took an image of him. . . . But of course someone did. He provided an image of himself in his own words. His parables and teachings tell us about him, but not according to appearance, which constantly alters in time, but according to his basic feelings, his basic personality and character, what the core of his being is, which does not alter, but remains constant. Teachings transcend time, even if appearances do not. The appearance we have of him is every human. Every human who seeks what every human is seeking: truth, love, contentment, security, happiness. Not knowing him visually, physically, but metaphysically, in our minds and thoughts and feelings, allows us to unite with him, see ourselves in him, and he in us. His physiognomy is spiritual, metaphysical, based on truth and love, not physical, and all that such physicality represents—the shallowness of humans, and their absurd focus on beauty, wealth, and power.

Other writers portraying other significant individuals of the past refused to describe their physical characteristics. Even so grand a writer as Homer portrayed his characters without distinct physical features—what Odysseus and Achilles looked like escaped Homer, and us. Likewise, great leaders of the Hebrew past, writers of poetry of immense beauty such as David, observers of God's invisible majesty such as Moses, had their words and actions recorded in detail—but it was left to later artists such as Michelangelo to portray the physical beauty and grandeur that matched their souls.

Artists for two thousand years have painted countless portraits of Jesus as a child in Mary's arms, adored by the Magi, sitting among the teachers in Jerusalem, rising from the water after baptism, the Holy Spirit lighting upon him, healing the blind and the lepers, walking on water, calming the storm, feeding the five thousand, teaching from the mount, raising Lazarus from the dead, praying, arriving at Jerusalem seated on a donkey, experiencing the Passover meal with his disciples, being betrayed by Judas, being arrested, appearing before the Sanhedrin, appearing before Pilate, being scourged, carrying the cross, being crucified, rising from the tomb, appearing again to his disciples, ascending to heaven. His long hair and beard, kind eyes, flowing robes, pious countenance—all imaginary.

Artists used as their sources for such portrayals the same sources biographers and historians must use: the Gospels. In Matthew, Mark, Luke, and John, we find the actions of Jesus's life, his words, his godlike demeanor.

The *Gospel of Mark* is not the first in order of appearance in the New Testament but, according to modern biblical scholarship, the first written, circa 65, *Anno Domini*, by John Mark, friend of the disciple Peter and associate of the apostle Paul. Written for a Jewish and Gentile audience, the *Gospel of Mark* introduces Jesus of Nazareth as the Son of Man. The mystery of this self-proclamation is further heightened by Jesus's insistence that those whom he heals should not reveal his true nature as the Christ, the Son of God. The reasons for his reticence to be so identified is as unclear as his preference for the designation of Son of Man. The Gospel does not provide the birth stories that are found in Luke and Matthew, and indeed does not provide any biographical information except for a vague account of Jesus's ministry when he is a mature adult and near the end of his life. Mark provides a disjointed chronological narrative, broken into various episodes in the life of Jesus, related in isolated vignettes. The Gospel emphasizes Jesus as healer and as Messiah bringing forth the Kingdom of God.

The *Gospel of Mark* is the shortest of the gospels, introducing stories and events that the longer gospels of Matthew and Luke explicate in greater detail. The portrayal of Jesus in the *Gospel of Mark* is more human than the others, notwithstanding the numerous miracles this Gospel (as well as the other three) describe. The Jesus of the *Gospel of Mark* is not always certain (as when he claims no one, not even himself, knows when the Son of Man will return); he is afraid on the night of his betrayal in the Garden of Gethsemane; he is reluctant for word that he is the Messiah to spread throughout the land; and he tells homely, pastoral parables to illustrate his life, message, and purpose.

The *Gospel of Mark* is written in a simple Greek than can mask its power and profundity. For example, Mark 9: 30-37: In this passage Jesus leads the disciples through Galilee, teaching them that "The Son of man will be delivered into the hands of men, and they will kill him; and when he is killed after three days he will rise." The disciples, however, are blind to the real purpose of Christ: "they did not understand the saying, and they were afraid to ask him." Uncertainty and secret fears of his words (*rhema*), which deal with last things (*eschatos*), lead them to a typical human response of fear, self-centeredness and narcissism. Coming to Capernaum, a port on the Sea of Galilee, the disciples discuss which one among them is greatest; Jesus castigates them for such vanity and tells them: "If any one would be first, he must be last of all and servant of all." Jesus knows that to act against fear and uncertainty one must turn to others, become a servant (*diakonos*) to others. The last will be first (*protos*). Then, "he took a child, and put him in the midst of them; and taking him in his arms, he said to them, 'Whoever receives one such child in my name receives me; and whoever receives me, receives not me but him who sent me.'" In short, to be like the prototype, Christ, one must embrace fear of last things, of death, and by serving others put aside fear.

German scholars of the nineteenth century believed that the reason Matthew and Luke have similar stories to Mark, often more fully rendered, is because Matthew and Luke relied on Mark as a basis for their Gospels. The stories of Jesus in Matthew and Luke not found in Mark, these German scholars reasoned, were based on another source, or common oral tradition, which they labeled *quelle* (source), or simply Q.

The *Gospel of Matthew*, written (probably) circa 70 *Anno Domini*, reputedly by a former tax collector and disciple of Christ identified in Luke and Mark as Levi, was directed toward Jewish Christians, to show Jesus was the Hebrew Messiah, fulfilling Hebrew prophecy. Matthew's most powerful statement in this regard is the Beatitudes, which reveal Jesus's knowledge of, and departure from, Hebrew teachings. Unlike the Ten Commandments—the Hebrew Law as a whole—the Beatitudes praise certain traits and behaviors rather than condemn specific actions. The verses following the Beatitudes are more severe injunctions of correct behavior. Jesus commands his listeners not only against killing, as in the Ten Commandments, but against anger and slander as well. Not only must a person not commit adultery, but also to refrain from looking at another person in lust, which is akin to adultery. Rather than "an eye for an eye, a tooth for a tooth," Jesus commands his followers to not resist violence with violence. "If any one strikes you on the right cheek, turn to him the other also." These are moral demands that cannot be met in normal everyday life, just like no one can completely abide by the Ten Commandments.

The *Gospel of Luke* was written circa 70, *Anno Domini*, by the physician Luke, Paul's friend, for an audience of Gentile Christians. This gospel presents the most full biographical account of Christ's life. Indeed Luke, who also wrote the *Acts of the Apostles*, was the first historian of Christianity, narrating the history of Jesus and his followers from Christ's birth to the activities of Paul throughout the Mediterranean region. Luke's Gospel, like Matthew and Mark, is often a disjointed series of vignettes. Jesus is the Son of Man who performs miracles and constantly warns that unbelievers and sinners will never see the Kingdom of God. Luke also provides the fullest account of the birth of Jesus, including the story of Joseph and Mary traveling to Bethlehem, finding no room for Mary who soon will give birth, finding a barn and a manger to lay the newborn in, and being visited by shepherds who have heard of the birth from angels. Luke provides the fullest account of the birth of John the Baptist. It is through Luke that we learn the most about the role of Mary in God's plan of redemption. Luke also provides the only information about Jesus in the years between his birth and ministry, when he is found conversing with scholars of the Jewish Law at the Temple in Jerusalem when he is twelve years old. In Luke, we have some of the most beautiful and most powerful stories and parables in the Gospel literature.

The first three Gospels of the New Testament are called the

Synoptic Gospels because they generally follow the same pattern and provide a similar account of Jesus. The fourth Gospel, John, is quite different. The *Gospel of John* was written circa 95, *Anno Domini*, by the disciple whom Jesus loved, John son of Zebedee. Written for Jewish Christians, it is the most mystical of the Gospels, heavily influenced by Greek philosophy. The *Gospel of John*, unlike the Synoptic Gospels, presents Jesus as the *logos*, the spoken, universal truth. John, by referring to Jesus as the *logos*, claims that Jesus is more than the Son of God and the Messiah: Jesus is eternally present, the light, knowledge itself, God manifested in His word. The *Gospel of John* presents the first coherent view of the Trinity: God the Father, Jesus the Son, and the Holy Spirit (the *paraclete* or advocate), of the same substance, the same being, but acting in different ways.

Jesus as presented by John is firmly God. He claims as much, as when he says to the Pharisees of Jerusalem (8: 58), "Truly, truly, I say to you, before Abraham was, I am." Such is the name of Yahweh ("I am Who I am"—*Exodus* 4: 14). Indeed, throughout the *Gospel of John*, Jesus claims "I am." "While I am in the world, I am the light of the world." (9: 5) "I am the gate for the sheep." (10: 7) "I am the good shepherd." (10: 11) "I am the resurrection and the life." (11: 25) "I am in the Father and the Father in me." (14: 11) "I am the true vine." (15: 1) "I am the bread of life." (6: 35) "I am the Way, the Truth, and the Life." (14: 6)

The Apostle Paul, also, in his *Epistles* in the New Testament, provides a metaphysical interpretation of Jesus as the Christ, the mystical Son of God. In his letters Paul, based his own experiences, portrays Christ as the all-encompassing God.

As a Pharisee, Paul was an expert on the Old Testament, the *Law*. He knew the prohibitions and restrictions and demands upon behavior and habit that permeated the *Pentateuch* as well as other books of the Bible. The Law informed humans how to live their lives to conform to God's will. The Pharisee Paul did just that, following the Law to conform to God's will. But his many efforts brought him to a startling conclusion: he could never live up to the strictures of the Law, and the effort to try to do so made him extremely unhappy. The rules of the Law and the nature of human behavior simply did not mix. Paul knew what was right and good; his reason told him that the Ten Commandments were important to obey. The problem was that Paul could never quite obey all the commandments. How can someone constantly, day by day, avoid coveting a neighbor's property, or disobeying parents, or baring false witness against another? It is impossible. The Law, an ideal that the reality of human existence can never match, made Paul miserable: the will, the desires of the body, always come to dominate the mind, the logic and reason that indicates how one *should* behave. Will limits Reason. Bodily experiences, temporal experiences, the search but inability to *know*, are the fruits of sin. Paul sought to will his behavior by planning how he would act in the future. But his bodily sensations, his movement through time, the constant passing moments, his ignorance about what the future would truly bring, save death, left him without direction, without purpose. Life seemed to be a moment by moment experience of failure that led to ignorance, fear, sickness, and death. How could such misery be avoided?

    Rubbing salt into the wound of sin was the reality of God's characteristics, which are completely opposite to human. God is timeless, all-knowing, pure Reason, the Truth. No gulf can be greater than that between God and human. God is in a sense the Law, the perfection of which makes humans failures by comparison, frail and unhappy. Only God can reconcile this apparent dilemma. To Paul, this was the mission of Jesus of Nazareth. *The word became flesh.* God bridged the gap by becoming human, being born of a virgin, experiencing life, time, despair, temptation, ignorance, pain, and death. The *incarnation* meant that Jesus, the *Son of Man*, experienced all human experiences, symbolized and became *Man* himself. As one man, Adam, symbolized the fall of man—the human experience of time, ignorance, and sin—so one man, Jesus, symbolized the elevation, life, joy, happiness, and release from the bonds of sin of all humans. Jesus died, but was resurrected in bodily form, as a distinct living being; hence all humans would be as well.

The literary portrait of the *Son of Man* is based on other direct sources as well. Matthew, Mark, Luke, John, Paul, and other Christians of the first century, *Anno Domini*, had a stake in what they were writing about—no one would believe their words unless they believed that Jesus had lived, was the Messiah, was God. The New Testament is an inherently biased source. The only non-Christian contemporary source for the life of Jesus was penned by the Jewish historian Flavius Josephus (37-100, *Anno Domini*). Josephus was a Pharisee, perhaps a member of the reclusive Essene sect that lived about the Dead Sea, a military leader in the uprising against the Romans that occurred in the 60s, *Anno Domini*, and eventually a turncoat who abandoned his countrymen for the Roman cause. He spent the last decades of his life in Rome in retirement, writing books for a Roman audience, in which he justified Rome's role in destroying Jerusalem and his own role in abandoning the Jewish cause. He changed his name from Joseph ben Matthias to Flavius Josephus, divorced his wife and married a Roman, and otherwise abandoned his heritage to live a luxurious life in Rome. Josephus was a Jew, perhaps even a pagan, but not a Christian. Josephus had no reason to write about Jesus save that the incidents surrounding Jesus's life were intriguing and fascinating, and as a historian Josephus decided to include them in his history. There are many versions of Josephus's history preserved in different languages. The Rumanian and Russian edition, translated from Greek, includes accounts of John the Baptist and Jesus. The following description of Jesus from Josephus's *Jewish History* echoes what is written in the Gospels:

> It was at that time that a man appeared ... who ... worked such wonderful and amazing miracles that I for one cannot regard him as a man. . . . Everything that some hidden power enabled him to do he did by an authoritative word. . . . In many ways he broke the Law. . . . At the same time his conduct was above reproach. He did not need to use his hands: a word sufficed to fulfill his every purpose. Many of the common people flocked after him and followed his teaching. . . . As a rule he was to be found opposite the City on the Mount of Olives, where also he healed the sick. He gathered round him 150 assistants and masses of followers. When they saw his ability to do whatever he wished by a word, they told him that they wanted him to enter the city, destroy the Roman troops, and make himself king; but he took no notice. When the suggestion came to the ears of the Jewish authorities, they met under the chairmanship of the high priest. . . . and told Pilate, who ... had the Miracle-worker brought before him, held an inquiry, and expressed the opinion that he was a benefactor, not a criminal or agitator or a would-be king. Then he let him go, as he had cured Pilate's wife. . . . When the crowds grew bigger than ever, he earned by his actions an incomparable reputation. The exponents of the Law were mad with jealousy, and gave Pilate 30 talents to have him executed. Accepting the bribe, he gave them permission to carry out their wishes themselves. So they seized him and crucified him.[3]

Josephus learned enough about the life of Jesus to know that he was someone with a reputation for divine or superhuman qualities; that he performed miracles and was a healer; that he had followers who expected him to overthrow the Roman occupation of Palestine; that the Jewish authorities considered him a liability in their relations with Rome; that he met with Pilate, who found him innocent but ultimately caved into Jewish pressure; that he was crucified.

The image of the Son of Man can also be reconstructed by means of the Hebrew Bible, which Jesus knew so well and upon which he modeled his life and teachings. The Psalms, for example, formed a part of him. Who precisely God is and what are His powers and interest in humans is made specifically clear in the Psalms. Largely written by David, the verse express piety and love, fear, search for redemption, need for deliverance.

Many Psalms use the imagery of a pastoral people. God is pictured as a shepherd to his sheep, the humans. Hence Psalm 23 reads:

> The Lord is my Shepherd, I shall not want;
> He makes me lie down in green pastures.
> He leads me beside still waters;
> He restores my soul.

The people of the Psalms live close to nature, to the desert lands and surrounding mountains. They look to Zion, the "holy mountain" in Psalm 15, hoping to "encamp" there, knowing that God will welcome persons who walk "spotless and practice righteousness," a person who speaks "truth in his heart." The psalmist flees from his enemies, like a bird in flight, soaring high to the mountains, where he finds God and can look upon His face. The God of Zion controls, crushes, overwhelms, blesses.

God serves mercy and justice. God might be distant from us, says Psalm 112, but He concerns himself with us, even the most lowly, even the poor, even the one on the dung heap, He raises up to be like a king. He brings fruit to the barren; He brings life to what hitherto has none. The chaff of evil blows in the wind, but the seeds of the good take root next to flowing waters. Listen to the Lord, listen to what He wants, deny the self for His will. Accept the will of God, fear the Lord, for to fear the Lord is to find wisdom.

The Psalms also express a yearning for God to avenge David against his enemies. Psalm 52 identifies the sinful ways of the enemy, which contrast with God's ways; surely God will punish them and reward the faithful.

> Why do you boast, O mighty man,
> Of mischief done against the godly?
> All the day you are plotting destruction.
> Your tongue is like a sharp razor,
> You worker of treachery.
> You love evil more than good,
> And lying more than speaking the truth.
> You love all words that devour,
> O deceitful tongue.

The depth of David's Psalms is such that they can often be read, as in this case, as being directed, rather than against an enemy, inward against the self. The psalmist condemns himself as the mighty man, his mischief against the kindness of God, the plotting of destruction (of self, not others), his sharp tongue and evil ways. His deceitful tongue focuses on the immediate, on grasping from each moment life, power, and vanity, even as one plummets toward death. The real punishment for his actions is simply death. The alternative is humility. God will break down this evil man, snatch him from his tent (of self-satisfaction). And notwithstanding the man's attempts to the contrary, to escape the future of death by wielding power, death will come nevertheless. The man seeks refuge in his riches, in his self, in his destructive ways, but such are things of a day and foreign to God. The option here is for the man to wait patiently upon the Lord (not the self), trust in God (not the self), get rid of arrogance and hubris, and accept the will of God and His offer of ultimate peace.

Non-canonical early Christian writers of the first four centuries, *Anno Domini*, also portrayed the Son of Man. These writings include the *Nag Hammadi Scrolls*, particularly the *Gospel of Thomas*. The papyrus and parchment *Nag Hammadi Scrolls* were discovered at Nag Hammadi, Egypt, in 1947. They contain a collection of writings from a sect of Christians heavily influenced by the Greek philosophy of Gnosticism, which assumed that truth involved the search for *gnosis*, inner knowledge, which is found within each person. Gnostic Christians believed that truth is spiritual rather than bodily, hence the search for God must involve an approach that transcends bodily experiences. Gnostic Christians such as Valentinus did not accept the orthodox interpretation of Christ's life that included the Incarnation, where God chose to take on human flesh and become man; the Crucifixion, where God chose to suffer and die; and the Resurrection, where God rose again in the flesh. Gnostics believed that flesh was evil, and that Jesus was not a bodily human, rather a spiritual presence, even on the Cross. This interpretation of Christ robbed Christianity of the central tenet that Christ must experience humanity to die for human sins, and was condemned as a heresy by the emerging Roman Catholic Church.

The Nag Hammadi corpus is a diverse collection of works. It includes new gospels, such as the *Gospel of Thomas, Gospel of Philip,* and *Gospel of Mary*; supposed works of other disciples, such as the *Apocryphon of James,* the *Apocryphon of John,* the *Apocalypse of James,* the *Apocalypse of Peter,* the *Letter of Peter to Philip,* and the *Act of Peter*; and other works of Christians, such as the *Prayer of the Apostle Paul* and the *Apocalypse of Paul.* Most of these works were undoubtedly known to early Christians, but were branded as heretical by early Church Fathers, and not included in the corpus that make up the New Testament. Modern scholars consider most of them to have been written several centuries after Christ's death, and reflect the thinking of second and third century Gnostic Christians, rather than the actual writings of the disciples and followers of Christ of the first century. There are, however, a few exceptions. The most important is the *Gospel of Thomas.*

The *Gospel of Thomas* is a Coptic translation of an original Greek text, with some indication that the sayings were originally in Aramaic, the spoken language of the Near East, hence of Jesus and His disciples. The gospel is a *sayings* gospel, that is, there are no biographical details, rather just the sayings of Jesus, most beginning with the statement, "Jesus said..." Modern scholarship places many of the sayings in the first century, *Anno Domini,* hence as old as the four canonical gospels. Some of the sayings are found in the four gospels, but others are completely new, and apparently authentic—that is, part of an oral tradition of the mid-first century that circulated the sayings of Jesus. The *Gospel of Thomas* is an extremely important source to understand Jesus and his teachings.

The *Gospel of Thomas* opens with the statement: "These are the secret sayings which the living Jesus spoke and which Didymos Judas Thomas wrote down." Thomas was the disciple known as the twin, in some traditions Jesus's twin; he was the "doubting" Thomas of the *Gospel of John*. The *Gospel of Thomas* confidently declares that "Whoever finds the interpretation of these sayings will not experience death." The *Gospel of Thomas* was doubtless included in the Gnostic corpus of the *Nag Hammadi Scrolls* because it has Gnostic overtones, such as the following: "The kingdom is inside you," Jesus said, "and it is outside of you. When you come to know yourselves, then you will become known, and you will realize that it is you who are the sons of the living father. But if you will not know yourselves, you dwell in poverty and it is you who are that poverty." Self-knowledge, *gnosis*, is the key, therefore, to the wealth of the Kingdom of Heaven. Many of the statements Jesus makes in the *Gospel of Thomas* are similar to those of the four Gospels, but others are quite different, such as: "Jesus said, 'When you see one who was not born of woman, prostrate yourselves on your faces and worship him. That one is your father.'" A Gnostic would not believe in the Virgin birth of Christ. Another Gnostic saying Jesus makes in the *Gospel of Thomas* is: "I shall give you what no eye has seen and what no ear has heard and what no hand has touched and what has never occurred to the human mind." Still another: "When you make the two one, and when you make the inside like the outside and the outside like the inside, and the above like the below, and when you make the male and the female one and the same, so that the male not be male nor the female female; . . . then will you enter [Heaven]." The *Gospel of Thomas* repeats some of the sayings of the Beatitudes, but adds a few new ones, such as: "Blessed is the man who has suffered and found life" and "Blessed are the hungry, for the belly of him who desires will be filled." Echoing the *Gospel of John*, Jesus says: "It is I who am the light which is above them all. It is I who am the all. From me did the all come forth, and unto me did the all extend."[4]

The *Son of Man* is the *all*, says Thomas: all of what? All of man, all of humanity. Jesus was most fully human. All for which a human seeks meaning he had realized and discovered in himself. Jesus was fully self-contained, that is, he lacked nothing, he was not incomplete, psychologically, emotionally, in any way. He overcame sin—lust, ignorance, pain, foreboding, incompleteness, loneliness—not by a miracle, simply by refusing to be overwhelmed and distracted by deception and fear. He found contentment, self-realization, freedom, by breaking from the deception of sin, the distractions of the moment, to find in the moment what is transcendent, what sums all moments: love.

The *Son of Man* has empathy toward all humans, which allows him to heal all, know all, sense all, fulfill expectations and imaginations, anticipate and interpret, encompass all human emotions, aspirations, and temporal experiences.

Each person contains the *Son of Man*, which is the definition of that mysterious phrase. Each life is precious not only for its own sake but also because it contains the image of the *Son of Man*. To sense his presence within is to find peace.

16

TRUTH

You shall know the truth and the truth shall set you free...

"Jesus of Nazareth, the King of the Jews." Written in Greek, Latin, and Hebrew, such was the title carved on the cross upon which Jesus of Nazareth was crucified, according to the *Gospel of John*.

"Are you the King of the Jews?" So asked Pontius Pilate after the Jews had brought Jesus to the Roman Praetorium, the official residence of the Procurator, requesting Pilate to condemn Jesus for unspecified charges. Jesus had been arrested the night before, betrayed by his disciple Judas; the Jews had interrogated him at the home of the high priest, accusing him of blasphemy. The four Gospel accounts differ in relating the story of Jesus's arrest, appearance before Pilate, scourging, and crucifixion. In the fourth *Gospel of John*, Pilate's first words to Jesus was the question, an apparent reference to the claim of Jesus's disciples that he was the Christ, the Messiah. Jesus, wondering that Pilate would ask him about kingship, responded, "Do you say this of your own accord, or did others say it to you about me?" The Roman Procurator, governor of Judaea, did not expect the accused to ask him a question, and responded, "Am I a Jew? Your own nation and the chief priests have handed you over to me; what have you done?" Jesus now responded to Pilate's initial question, saying: "My kingship is not of this world; if my kingship were of this world, my servants would fight, that I might not be handed over to the Jews; but my kingship is not from the world." To this confusing response, Pilate asked, "So you are a king?" Jesus responded, again unexpectedly: "You say that I am a king. For this I was born, and for this I have come into the world, to bear witness to the truth. Every one who is of the truth hears my voice." Pilate, bewildered, responded: "What is truth?"

Pilate was confused indeed. Not only did the interview with the strange man dressed like a commoner confuse him, but, as Pilate's question revealed, *truth* itself confused him. The Roman world of the first century, *Anno Domini*, had numerous philosophic and religious options that professed to teach the truth. The accounts of Pilate in the New Testament reveal little about his beliefs, save that he was a pragmatist concerned only with preserving his own power. He had his appointment as Procurator from the emperor Tiberius, who succeeded Augustus and ruled Rome from 14 to 37, *Anno Domini*. Tiberius, indeed most of the early Roman *princeps* and emperors, concerned themselves with power and position rather than ideas. Roman philosophy, such as it was, derived from the Greeks, whose ideas and systems of thought were multifaceted, ranging from an acceptance of grand metaphysical ideas to questioning and doubt. Few Romans embraced the ideas of the Academicians, a school of thought deriving from the teachings of Socrates and Plato, focusing on universal concepts rarely experienced by humans, who only know the shadows of what is real. Likewise the Peripatetic school, founded by Aristotle, focused exclusively on reason and inductive thinking, which Romans such as Pilate typically found unappealing. Roman men of action in the military and government, interested in substantive ideas, found the materialist philosophies of the Stoics and Epicureans more consistent with their habits and concerns. Although the Epicurean and Stoic philosophies derived from the Greeks as well, these philosophers eschewed metaphysics for a belief system of the here and now. Epicureans, for example, concerned themselves with the avoidance of pain and the increase of pleasure. Many Romans agreed with the first century, *Ante Christos*, Epicurean philosopher Lucretius, who argued that the divine, if it exists, is irrelevant, that the universe is comprised of particles, atoms, in constant motion, which form all reality, and which have neither a beginning nor an end. The Stoics had a similar belief in the atomic theory of reality, believing that the spiritual does not exist, per se, that all ideas, thoughts, divinity are composed of atoms in diverse and infinite combinations. Stoics essentially believed that only life, the here and now, is relevant, and that one must pursue the means to achieve contentment in the present, ignoring what is to come and moving beyond what has happened. Stoics could be impatient with grand ideas of the truth, hence Pilate's question to Jesus could have revealed a bit of the Stoic in him, save that the Stoics had a belief in a divine material force, the *logos*, which harked back to Greek metaphysical ideas, and could have made a pragmatist such as Pilate very uncomfortable. Pilate's uncertainty about truth might have indicated that he was a Skeptic, a Greek philosophy that had many Roman adherents. Skeptics were so unsure about what is real and true that they suspended judgment, refusing to accept answers to the many questions, content merely to question, to consider possibilities, without ever embracing a particular belief. Pilate's question perhaps simply implied that he did not believe truth existed, that he was *cynical* of any system of thought that attempted to find order in chaos, reason in folly. Otherwise he might have been more intrigued by Jesus's claims to be the *king of truth*. Rather, Pilate rejected any transcendental truth, rejected Jesus, rejected the religion of the Jews, and in derision crucified Jesus as the King of the Jews, knowing that nothing could be more absurd than Jesus being a king or that the Jews would accept such a person as king.

The tragedy of Pontius Pilate was that truth stared him in the face but he waved it aside for the sake of appearance and security. Jesus was obviously not a king in the traditional sense, but the world of the first century, *Anno Domini*, had other expressions of kingship about which an educated Roman such as Pilate might have known. Although the Jews of Jerusalem had recently, before Pilate, had kings, the Herods ruling them, it was not by choice, rather by compulsion: the Jews had rejected kingship in all of its forms for centuries, and rebelled against foreign kings when opportunity presented itself. The Romans worked with kings when necessary, but likewise themselves eschewed kingship, having rebelled against kings five hundred years before; Julius Caesar was assassinated when he tried to establish himself as a king; and the emperors, such as Augustus and Tiberius, held *imperium*, power derived by conquest, but not *royal* power. The Greeks were more accommodating to notions of monarchy, and Greek kings had until the previous centuries controlled Egypt, Macedonia, and Greek-Asia. Greek thinkers enjoyed cogitating about the philosopher-king, which became a model, in time, for Roman emperors, such as Hadrian and Marcus Aurelius. Jesus was obviously a philosopher rather than a king, and doubtless Pilate sensed what Jesus meant when he claimed to be a *king of truth* (*aletheias*). Likewise when Pilate informed Jesus that he had the power to release or crucify him, Jesus's response, that Pilate did not inherently have such power over life and death, which was an authority beyond the power of men, was very much akin to the arguments of Greek philosophers, from Socrates to Seneca, that no other human has power over oneself—only the self controls the self.

Jesus's brief interview with Pilate, then, was sufficient for the Roman to realize the depth of the Jew's philosophy, which was not very different from that of the Greeks and Romans. The New Testament, the only source for the philosophy and beliefs of Jesus, reveals a Greco-Roman and Hebrew worldview that accepts and reflects many of the ideas and assumptions of the society and culture of the Greeks and Romans. Evidence for the importance of Greek culture in Jesus's world comes from the *Septuagint*, the Hebrew Bible translated into Greek by Alexandrian Jews in the wake of the conquests of Alexander the Great. Many of the books of the Hebrew Bible had Greek influence, for example *Ecclesiastes*, in which the *teacher* declares that "what has been is what will be, and what has been done is what will be done; and there is nothing new under the sun," with which many Greek philosophers of the Hellenistic period were in total agreement. Likewise, the teacher's comment that "in much wisdom is much vexation, and he who increases knowledge increases sorrow," is a perfect fit for classical humanistic thought. The apocryphal *Book of Wisdom*, written in Greek by an Alexandrian Jew less than a century before the birth of Christ[1], anticipates the "righteous man" being tortured and killed by those who believe that there is nothing beyond life; they are unaware, however, that

> the souls of the righteous are in the hand of God, and no torment will ever touch them. In the eyes of the foolish they

seem to have died, and their departure was thought to be an affliction, and their going from us to be their destruction; but they are at peace.[2]

This notion that death is a release of the soul, the spirit, is found in latter Jewish thought as well as in many religious expressions of the Mediterranean world. Greek Gnostic thought, as found in the *Nag Hammadi Scrolls*, was very mystical, and akin to such writers as John, author of the fourth Gospel and three epistles in the New Testament. Indeed, John's concept of the *logos*, and the Apostle Paul's metaphysical interpretation of Christ, fit neatly with the philosophy behind many of the Greek mystery religions, the new Platonic thought (Neoplatonism) of the first few centuries, *Anno Domini*, and the Stoic interpretation of *logos*, seen in the philosophy of Marcus Aurelius (*Meditations*). One of the reasons for the spread of Christianity throughout the Roman Empire was that the New Testament was composed in spoken Greek, *koine*, the *lingua franca* of the Mediterranean world. The Gospels, recording the conversation between Pilate and Jesus, would have us believe they conversed in Greek.

The idea of *truth*, then, was not unfamiliar to Pilate—indeed truth appeared in dozens of forms during his time of the first century, *Anno Domini*. Even Jesus's comment that his was the *voice* (Greek *phones*) *of truth* would be familiar to a relatively educated person. The idea of a spoken truth was familiar to Hebrews, Greeks, and Romans. Old Testament writers such as Isaiah portrayed God, *the truth*, speaking to humans in the mind and auditorily as well. Jesus, according to the *Gospel of John*, declared to his disciples that after his death an advocate, the "spirit of truth," would come and "speak" to them. Greco-Roman philosophers also conceived of the spoken truth, the *word* or *logos*, an expression of being, the source of the universal transcendence. The *logos* was a central idea of the Stoics, the most popular philosophy in the Roman Empire.

Humans run from the truth. Fear and avoidance rather than acceptance, pain rather than pleasure, is the typical human response to the voice of truth. Pilate's defining characteristic in the passion of Christ was fear: of the Jews, of the emperor, of the crowd, of Jesus, of the truth—a *legion* of fear. Fear is the defining characteristic of all people, save Jesus, in the New Testament. All of Jesus's disciples feared him and his truth. Those who did not understand him feared him. The Jews feared him and sought to kill him. The persecutor Saul, become the Apostle Paul, feared him. Perhaps the only people who did not fear him were those, like Legion, whom Jesus had healed.

IV

THE LEGION OF FEAR VANQUISHED

He came in the darkness of ignorance and despair, at the abyss of the unseen, when the faint colors of dawn hint at what will be, yet all is quiet and still save the ruminating mind bringing forth disaster and dissolution. He came unexpectedly in response to a petition surging forth from desperation. He came in answer to prayer. He made his physical presence known and the whole form of man shuttered. He came in an instant, stayed but an instant. But the change was irreversible. He came to still the fear, end the terror, stop the pain, quiet the mind. He came to instill hope, peace, love. He shattered time and the will, revealed and implanted the transcendent, and formed all eternity out of the single moment. The word became flesh and thundered forth, concise and articulate, its meaning unmistakable, its voice irrefutable, its impact permanent. A thousand ideas, countless experiences, dictionaries of terms and encyclopedia of examples, reached an apogee in a single word. Be still, be at peace, yield, surrender, embrace, trust. Know that I am. Receive what you do not understand. Accept

17

THE CONTINUING PRESENCE OF FEAR

estroy this temple and in three day's I will raise it up...
After the death of Jesus upon the cross—after scourging, nails, and humiliation had done its work, he had breathed his last, and Pilate ensured that he was indeed dead—a rich man of the town of Arimathea, Joseph, braved an audience with Pilate, in which he asked for the body of Jesus. Joseph was not only wealthy, but a local leader, perhaps a member of the Sanhedrin, therefore would have been known to Pilate, who agreed to his request. John says that Joseph was one of Jesus's disciples, not the twelve, but the many others who followed him. John also says that Nicodemus, a member of the Sanhedrin as well, who had become a follower of Jesus, brought the traditional spices, myrrh and aloe, with which to anoint the dead. There was nearby on Golgotha a garden in which was a vacant tomb newly-hewn from rock. We can speculate without knowing why there was this vacant tomb available for Jesus, why Joseph requested the body, why Pilate agreed, and why Jesus's enemies did not try to prevent the burial. Matthew, Mark, and Luke agree that Jesus was laid in the tomb after having been wrapped in a shroud; John says he was anointed with the spices

then wrapped in the shroud. At the end of the day, the Sabbath began, and nothing further could be done until its conclusion.

Jesus was crucified on Friday and laid to rest; he stayed in the tomb until Sunday morning, when it was reported that he had risen. The four Gospel accounts provide different versions of how Mary Magdalene and other women went to the tomb to put spices on the body, even though a large rock sealed the tomb and, according to Matthew, soldiers guarded it. Mark and Luke say that the women went to the tomb not knowing who would remove the rock. John simply says that Mary Magdalene went to the tomb alone and found the rock removed. In all four Gospels, Jesus had left the tomb, though he was nearby, resurrected to life. None of the accounts provide any information as to when he left the tomb, how he was resurrected, how long he had been dead before he lived again, and whether or not any other force, such as angels, assisted him in this resurrection. Such details are perhaps hidden because of the miraculous nature of the event.

Time the tempter intervened in the lives of Jesus's disciples. Even when they learned that the tomb was empty, that he had risen, they allowed fear, doubt, uncertainty—time—to tempt them into inaction and disbelief.

Those days after his arrest and crucifixion seemed, to his followers, like a dream. The many accounts of the resurrection in the Gospels imply the confusion about what exactly happened. Matthew says that Jesus appeared to Mary Magdalene and "the other Mary," then later, at Galilee, on a mountain, to the disciples. Mark says that he appeared to Mary Magdalene, then to two men walking, then to the disciples. Luke does not mention the appearance to Mary but describes a long conversation the risen Jesus had with two disciples on the road to Emmaus, and that he appeared to Peter followed by all of the eleven disciples. John describes a conversation between the risen Jesus and Mary Magdalene, then his appearance that evening among the disciples, when he greeted them saying, "Peace be with you."

A few of the Gospel accounts imply doubt among some of the witnesses. With so many different rumors circling among his followers, doubt would be a secure place to fall back upon. The *Gospel of John* mentions the chief doubter by name, Thomas—Judas Thomas, the Twin (Didymus). The evening of the resurrection, Jesus appeared among the disciples in a house. Thomas was absent, and when they told him of the appearance, he replied: "Unless I see in his hands the print of the nails, and place my finger in the mark of the nails, and place my hand in his side, I will not believe."

Alive again? How? Why? What could it mean? How can the dead come back to life? Resist the truth. Doubt. Resist the horror of the past. Resist time, power, responsibility, mortality, contradiction, uncertainty, oppression, insignificance, ignorance, meaninglessness. It does not take a philosopher to peer into the future and see that violence, pain, suffering, oppression, humiliation, rape, murder, war, execution, manipulation, defeat, slaughter, imprisonment, crucifixion, and torture, await. Who can accept the horror of war, the deaths of countless innocents, the executions, the slaughter in cities, the cries of children, the victims of war? Who can accept the seemingly infinite list of crimes of one human upon another? Who can accept the natural disasters that permeate the harmony and grace of nature, that counter the wonder of life with violent and premature death? Resist, fight, avoid, escape.

Resistance yields questions upon questions. What can be order in chaos? Amid so much death and destruction where can one find life and peace? How can meaning be found in meaninglessness?

Eight days passed, according to John, during which Thomas doubted, which, since the passing days revealed no evidence of the miraculous visitation of the night of the resurrection, could have spread to others as well, especially to those who, like Thomas, had heard of the appearance, but had not experienced it themselves. Time is a destroyer of faith: day upon day, the passing moments, the fears of what will be, the uncertainty of thoughts and feelings, the hunger to know, the fatigue of the present, the drowsiness that persists amid startling truth. The world of dreams is most appealing, the fantasy of what has happened, what might have happened, what could have happened—as the days pass it becomes unclear, memory fades, erased by doubt: *Did it ever happen? Did I actually experience it? Did I see it? Feel it? If so, why has it gone away? Why is memory my only solace? Perhaps it was not real. Perhaps it was a wonderful dream. Perhaps what I feel now, nothing, is reality.*

Jesus blessed doubting Thomas with an appearance. He stood before Thomas, and said, "Put your finger here, and see my hands; and put out your hand, and place it in my side; do not be faithless, but believing." Thomas, astonished, rather than testing the vision by probing and feeling, replied in utter wonder and belief, "My Lord and my God!" Doubts vanished in a moment of awareness. It took visual evidence in time, rather than acceptance of the past experiences, to vanquish resistance in Thomas, at least for the present. Jesus, knowing the frivolity of human belief, the constant demand to see to believe, responded to Thomas: "Have you believed because you have seen me? Blessed are those who have not seen and yet believe."

Thomas saw the risen Jesus but did not touch him. Earlier, when Jesus appeared to Mary Magdalene, according to John, and she wished to embrace him, he told her not to, "for I have not yet ascended to the Father." Luke writes that he appeared among the disciples, and said: "Why are you troubled, and why do questionings rise in your hearts? See my hands and my feet, that it is I myself; handle me, and see; for a spirit has not flesh and bones as you see that I have." Luke does not write that the disciples touched him, though Jesus also asked them for something to eat. Mark is vague about Jesus's appearance, only saying that he appeared to Mary Magdalene, to two men, then to the eleven. Matthew says that Mary Magdalene and her companion saw Jesus, and embraced his feet. These varying accounts led to much confusion among later believers, who were not quite sure if Jesus appeared again in bodily form, truly alive, or as a spirit, an image of life. When one sees something, how can one determine its reality except by feeling, touching, embracing? The mind plays tricks, perhaps not at first, but later, when memory of the event, now passed, is fuzzy, and the reality of what was seen is in doubt.

There is no reason to choose: Jesus appeared to his followers in bodily and in spiritual form. Such is the experience of time, that it partakes of moments of mental and physical awareness. To only feel is insufficient. To only see is insufficient. An experience in the moment has to involve the mind and body. A dream has to be envisioned and felt. A vision has to be seen and touched. A voice has to register in the ears and not just the mind. The presence of God must embrace all: the shuttering of the body accompanying the images of the mind, the feeling of peace encompassing the whole—limbs, fingers, toes, as well as the inner self. The experience of time is never one or the other. The incarnation cannot be one or the other, either. God does not become man without leaving a physical remnant behind. God does not experience time without experiencing the whole of it—body, mind; pleasure, pain; joy, sorrow; life, death.

Death is not the end. As the accounts of the resurrection reveal, it is a beginning. But it is a beginning that is uncertain according to the standards of life and time. John ends his gospel with an account of the disciples in a boat fishing, seeing a person on the shore. They think it is the risen Jesus, but they cannot quite tell. He appears differently. He does not look the same. Jesus appears differently in each moment to those who still live in time, who still experience the passing moments. Blessed are those who have not seen yet believe. *Believe* is present tense. Break from past assumptions and the burden of the past and anticipation of the future. Break from the constraints of time. Right now, in the present, is when one knows—in the present, no deception. In the present, now, know. Blessed are those who no matter what has happened in the past believe, now.

18

THE VOICE OF A CHILD

ake it and Read...
The phrase *Anno Domini*, used to date events after the coming of Christ, has gone out of fashion, replaced by the pedestrian phrase *Common Era*. *Anno Domini* has been in use for centuries. Why? Because it is personal, refers to the Year of the Lord in one's own personal life. Personal time is increasingly trumped by the universality of digital clocks, atomic clocks, alarm clocks, clocks on television, on car dashboards, on cellphones—everywhere. Time has become a thing, an entity, rather like the economy, unable to understand, unable to control. This impersonal, artificial standard of measuring being comes to dominate the actions of people hourly, daily, weekly, monthly, yearly. Then it is all over; but what has it all meant? *Anno Domini* reveals that time is important as it relates to the person living it, not to someone else. The movement of days is completely personal to each human, who keeps a private diary in his/her head to trace its passing. It is not meant to be an exterior standard for measurement, to accommodate, to alter life for, to subject being to. It is an individual's relationship with God, the

Son of Man, whereby each moment is an invitation to interact with the divine, to find in life not a whole, not over time, but in each second, each minute, a dialogue with the transcendent, an opening to truth. This is what Jesus taught. This is what Paul wrote about. This is what Aurelius Augustine experienced.

Aurelius Augustine was a fourth-century skeptic, like Paul, an apostate who laughed at the stories found in the Bible; he knew that, compared to the great philosophies of his time, the ancient world, the miracles and healings of the New Testament were infantile. But then he heard the *Voice of a Child*.

Augustine's thought matured during the late fourth century when the Roman Empire staggered under a series of internal and external blows. Internally, centuries of civil war had taken its toll on manpower, the Greco-Roman city, thought and culture, and the general sense of well-being of the individual Roman. Autocratic emperors had removed any vestiges of once Republican Rome. Slavery and serfdom were on the rise. Cities were places of vice and filth. At the same time a variety of less "civilized" peoples on Rome's borders sought to enjoy the wealth, infrastructure, and civilization of the Roman Empire. Parthians to the east, Germanic tribes to the north, and Numidians and Berbers to the south put constant, unrelenting pressure on the borders of the Empire. At various times these peoples pierced holes, as it were, in the armor of the Empire's defenses. One such occasion was the Battle of Adrianople in 378, when Roman emperor Valens died at the hands of the invading Goths.

In 410, the unthinkable occurred, when Goths under Alaric entered and sacked the city of Rome, which had been spared such violence for eight hundred years. Romans wondered what were the causes of such catastrophes plaguing the Empire. Pagans argued that the reason for Rome's troubles was the abandonment of the worship of the traditional gods, such as

Jupiter, whose anger was bringing the Empire to a halt. The Christians were to blame for substituting a new religion for the traditional beliefs of early Rome. The Christian bishop of the city of Hippo in North Africa, Aurelius Augustine, took exception to these attacks on Christianity. He decided to write a book in response. The *City of God* became one of the great religious treatises of all time, and provided a clear answer to the question, *What caused the Fall of Rome?*

Aurelius Augustine's answer was twofold. On a grand scale of human history, he argued that there are two cities, the City of Man and the City of God. The former is corrupt, filled with fear, sinful, the heir to the original sin of Adam; the latter is timeless, fearless, eternal, untouched by sin and evil. The former City of Man, humans and their institutions, will never succeed at approaching the absolute truth and harmony of the City of God while on this earth and subject to the consequences of sin. Just as the body slowly ages and decays and death awaits all humans, likewise human institutions—such as the Roman Empire—age, decay, and die. Romans often referred to the city of Rome as the Eternal City; but this is completely false, Augustine argued, for nothing created by human hands can be eternal. Rome, then, is destined to fall, just as all empires, all institutions, all human creations, each human, is destined to fall, to die. Live life with your eyes on the City of God, and await your destiny, after death, of becoming a citizen of that Eternal City.

How precisely does one become a citizen of the Eternal City of God? Augustine used the story of life, in this case his own, to find the answer. Introspective even when growing up in the North African city of Thagaste, arrogance and vanity compelled him to reject his mother Monica's Christian teachings to pursue success and fame as a scholar and orator. Sin drove him to unhappiness even as he sought happiness through philosophy.

Cicero and Roman Stoicism had an early influence on Augustine, who found appealing the Stoic notions of *humanitas*: a common humanity, equality, and the dignity of humankind. The Stoics emphasized human experience as the key to happiness, but all of Augustine's attempts to unlock the door failed. During these years of his late teens and twenties Augustine was a materialist who, when Stoicism could not provide sufficient answers, sought elsewhere. The words of his autobiography, *Confessions*, exudes the pain of recollection that he strayed so far as to embrace an eastern materialistic philosophy, Manicheism. Augustine sought from the Manicheists an explanation of the pain, fear, and sorrow that he felt, the evil within him. The Manicheist solution was simple: evil has a material presence within oneself; likewise the material of good can be increased or decreased depending upon lifestyle. Manicheism, however, did not bring Augustine contentment.

In pursuit of success—in pursuit of truth—Augustine migrated to Rome, then to Milan, where he taught rhetoric. At Milan he came under the influence of the Bishop, Ambrose. Augustine admired Ambrose, who influenced Augustine to begin a reassessment of Christian scripture, which Augustine had long considered with disdain as filled with fantastic stories told ineloquently. But, Ambrose suggested and Augustine considered, what if the stories of the Old and New Testaments were allegories of more profound spiritual phenomena? Meanwhile Augustine read Neoplatonist philosophers such as Plotinus, who helped to convince Augustine that truth is spiritual not material, and that sin is not a substance but willful error in behavior.

Slowly, under the onslaught of the appeals of his mother, the sermons of St. Ambrose, and Neoplatonic arguments that reality is spiritual, Augustine turned to Christianity. He studied the

Scriptures, particularly the *Epistles* of the Apostle Paul. He found in Paul a rational theology of a mind equal to his own.

At this point living at Milan, wealthy, successful, and famous, understanding the contributions to human understanding of the Stoics, Neoplatonists, and Manicheists, deeply influenced by Ambrose and his own mother, Monica, Augustine now realized that his experiences were Paul's experiences. Paul, too, had been burdened by the reality of sin, the constant helpless recognition of his own willfulness and error, the overwhelming anxiety and fear that life brings. Notwithstanding his new awareness, Augustine found the struggle with the flesh defeated his desire for chaste living. Eventually sin and unhappiness drove him to a pinnacle of personal anguish where he sought the strength to control his temporal desires. While in the garden at the home of a friend, Augustine broke down into anxious tears during which he heard a child's voice cry, "Take it and read, take it and read." Augustine answered the child's call by turning to Paul's *Epistles* and reading the first passage upon which his eyes fell, which was Paul's comment, "Not in reveling and drunkenness, not in debauchery and licentiousness, not in quarreling and jealousy. But put on the Lord Jesus Christ, and make no provision for the flesh, to gratify its desires." The words hit home and Augustine was changed, born again.

What is most fascinating about his conversion experience was the child's voice. What *really* happened? Was it the wind? Was it Augustine's imagination? Perhaps it was his unconscious mind, the voice of fear and despair from his sinful youth. Upon hearing the voice Augustine's first response was to think "hard whether there was any kind of game in which children used to chant words like these"[1]—clearly it was an auditory event. But why a child's voice? Why not a blinding light or a booming expression of omnipotence? Notwithstanding Augustine's beliefs respecting original sin, a child represents innocence if for no other reason than that a child is beginning, newness, potential—and the future awaits. A child best represents humanity in its purity, for it is new to the world, and in its questioning, its wide-eyed wonder. It is not surprising that the Gospel writers Matthew and Luke began their stories of the life of Jesus with tales of his birth. Their message was that the Messiah was ever youthful, ever innocent, ever pure, ever simply human—uncorrupted, unmoved, by civilization. The child symbolizes the inherent equality and dignity of humanity; the child is a model of humanity, transcending time and place: what can be less unique, less an individual, than a newborn? Augustine's experience of the voice of the child was all things and more: imagination, the unconscious mind, the wind blowing, a thought and a memory, corporeal and auditory, distinctly heard in a passing instant. The voice was all the phenomena, events, thoughts, and feelings that make up an individual human—a transcendent occurrence in a single moment of time.

Aurelius Augustine, Paul of Tarsus, and the disciples Peter, John, and James heard the voice, the incarnation within them, the presence of Christ, the word become flesh. John learned that Christ is in all people, he is eternally present, and that the world could not hold all the books that could be written to describe his wonderful works—in other words, the world could not hold the book of life that exists for each and every person. Each person has the voice, each person has the word, and in each person there are miracles just like the turning of water into wine and the raising of Lazarus. Each person's life is a unique miracle, and has the basis of truth within, in one's own experiences, when one can come to find the *word* within oneself. Each person's life has the stuff to make up a Bible. The story of Jesus in the *Gospel of John* is the story of the *word* becoming flesh in each person—the

Gospel helps humans to recognize the significance and presence of Christ not only in the events of 2000 years ago but in the events of today, of now. For the same *word* is alive, has become flesh, in each person, even if most do not recognize it.

Notwithstanding what life brings, the sin, the violence, the darkness of humanity, humans treasure life because in the simplicity of life there is no darkness. Life can be short and brutish, but it is nevertheless life, filled with the glories of spring, the squeals of the infant, the smells of the harvest, heaping bowls of food, the beauties of the gentle rill, and romance under the full moon. Man knows woman, and woman knows man. Time, dates, age, years, are uncertain, but infancy, childhood, young adulthood, adulthood, and old age have remained the same as at the beginning. Hunger and famine have always been just around the corner, but also good harvests and a full stomach. The Son of Man appears not in radiant ornament, in soaring spires, in golden crosses, but in childbirth, on the deathbed, in lovemaking, through the toil of the day, in the few scattered moments of joy and peace, in the plentiful harvest and the cooling rains, and in the warm embrace.

Great philosophers have written great books describing what every person knows from simply living. But is *knowing* sufficient? How can knowledge be brought to bear on the actions of the everyday, on *living*? Paul had so many experiences in which he stared, as it were, into the eyes of Christ, and yet in daily living he was still bothered by the thorns of the flesh. *If I know God is present, that God is universal, His love and care are ubiquitous, then why am I not able to still the temptations and deceptions of the moment? Why am I not able to be still and rest in God? Why can I not rid myself of these nagging thorns of the flesh, brought by the deceiver, which distract me from what I know is true?* Paul, confused and impatient with sin, cried out to God: relieve me of these thorns! But, he says, God responded with a simple message: "My grace is sufficient for you."

God's grace is sufficient. Michel de Montaigne knew this: "To compose our character is our duty, not to compose books, and to win, not battles and provinces, but order and tranquillity in our conduct. Our great and glorious masterpiece is to live appropriately."[2] The idea that living can be a masterpiece, a work of art, is an old one in the Western Tradition: it is the sum of the thought of Epicurus and Zeno, Socrates and Plato, Livy and Cicero, Marcus Aurelius and Boethius, Augustine and Jesus. Contentment in the singular moment results from faith in, acceptance of, oneself; piety toward existence as well as toward its giver; and the historical awareness that one's life is at the same time one and the many, as a color in the whole spectrum of light, beautiful itself yet spectacular when combined with others.

Each person's final essay in life is one common to human experience, to all life. How one lives indicates how one will die. Indeed, life itself is enduring death, passage toward a certain end. The only question is the duration of the passage. Ironically it is when life is good and one feels happy in the morning sunshine and content in the coming of night that death is an easy companion. But the despair of ruminating thoughts on any of life's contingencies makes death burdensome. A person fears death most when a person hates life. "How many ways has death to surprise us!" Montaigne wrote. Its presence is constantly on the mind. *When I fall asleep something in me sees what it is like to die. When I wake I feel renewed, reborn, I live again.* Illness reminds a person of death, as do accidents, any contingent occurrence. Some people box death up deep inside them. But the ruminator cannot. The ruminator is always contemplating, analyzing, hypothesizing, searching: mind never at rest, awake at nights with new anxieties, new fears, recalling the past, anticipating the future. Something calls within, some hidden power bids, demands, that one's days be filled not with harmony but with conflict, daily battles, a war within, the struggle of feelings with ideas, of body with mind, of time with eternity. The ruminator imagines death when alive, sickness when healthy, hate when in love, sorrow when happy, destruction when complete.

Each person faces the wall of imminent death. Before scaling it a person must first fight back the image of destruction, of loss of control, of giving in to the inclination to die. To live until one dies requires so much will. One alternative is to turn to the wall and die. Another is to turn from the wall, existing in the shadow of the wall, refusing to accept, to live. Or, one can ascend the wall and the many others in its wake—and truly live.

We all have a cross to bear upon which our bodily experiences are nailed, our sides pierced with pain, the blood dripping from the open wounds of the collage of sensations that grip our minds. Hope and fear emerge simultaneously and wage battle. What if my faith is erroneous and there is no God, or God is unjust, that I am forsaken? What if my faith is true but my choices have been wrong, my life a crime of questioning and doubting, hubris rather than humility? What if God simply does not care, and leaves me to suffer and die alone?

Then the moment comes. The aching limbs, the thirst, the dizziness, the pain, the taunts of others, the wretched storms of the day, the darkness of the sky, the terrorizing lightning, the abandonment, the loneliness . . . renewed strength, the drink, the light of day, the vision, understanding, oneness, hope, non-movement, stillness, a single moment from which all is known.

19

I AM

Before Abraham was, . . . During the course of Jesus's long discourse concluding the sermon on the mount, as recorded by Matthew, Jesus proclaims: "You cannot serve God and Mammon." The things of a day, the daily items of clothing, shelter, possessions, and food, are necessary for survival but not sufficient for happiness. Food, shelter, and clothing are a means to an end, life, but alone each is not the object of life. Yet because of the narrowness of the human vision of *what is*, the acquisition and use of material goods for clothing, sustenance, comfort, entertainment, and pride become the end. *Get behind me, Satan,* Jesus was wont to say, perhaps on a daily basis. The evil of each day is the temptation of each moment, which builds into a crescendo of moments, hours, days, in which all a person thinks about is food, clothing, possessions, and luxury. These *get us through* to the end of the day, or *tide us through* to the weekend, when the cycle continues again, never ending. There are various forms of temptation, of course: not just food, clothing, and possessions, but lust, fame, power, security, order, contentment, happiness. A person can be as tempted by the illusion of contentment as by the illusion of riches; fooled into a sense of security when disorder and danger await, just outside oneself. Each moment tempts with what can be rather than what is. The restlessness brought by the passing moments is the human curse. The inability to hold the moment still is its inherent evil. Jesus said that this moment to moment anxiety is folly, as it will not feed or clothe or make a person better whether a person worries about what happens next or simply lets it happen. Life will still be life no matter if it is dressed up or called something different. Humans are, in the end, simply naked, as are the birds of the air and the flowers of the field. God provides for all. Humans rarely feel that what they have been provided is enough. But if the soil and rain and sunshine is enough for the lily, and the air, seed, nesting trees, and a place to rest is enough for birds, then *life*, what God has provided, is enough.

Time ends. All things come to a halt. Death is when a person becomes still, and movement stops. Knowledge and life are based on said movement; death brings a different state of being, unrecognizable to those still alive. It is natural to fear the unknown. Death is unknown to those who are alive, hence it is the greatest fear. We fear the end. We fear nonexistence. We fear not being. We fear not knowing who we are. We fear the world without us. We fear dissolving, decaying, into something unrecognizable. We fear a future of death.

Humans experience time moment by moment—the sequential experiences of gain, loss, hunger, fullness, pain, pleasure, anger, pleasantness, loneliness, togetherness, lust, satisfaction, fear, courage. These sequential experiences sometimes almost, or do, overwhelm us, captivate us, scare us, make us think of little else than our immediate needs. Such was the experience of Legion. He wondered, what is there in the immediate needs that involves God, eternity, peace, happiness? Where is transcendent truth, God, in momentary concerns?

Humans, unable to hold still the moment, seek truth according to the continuity of passing moments. Each moment in and of itself hardly yields truth, but we glimpse truth by means of the continuous experiences of common truth that seem to transcend the individual moment. Present awareness combined with recollection of the past and anticipation of the future, directed toward those experiences that we find meaningful, are the bases for the truth that we experience. The continuity of moment by moment experience is a means to sense transcendent truths. The past-present-future continuum is the only route to know God, for continuity shows us that each moment is not meaningless, indeed each moment provides a glimpse of the one moment in which God exists, which is *still*. The path to knowledge and truth is through trying to figure out the continuity of fleeting moments.

Humans have known this key to transcending time for millennia; the techniques to transcend time have changed. To break away from the selfish concerns of life, to break away, therefore, from the dependence on the solitary moment, fits with the belief systems of many other world philosophies and religions. For example, Buddhists argue that one must deny one's carnal urges to be able to approach Nirvana, which is the breaking away from Self. Stoics believe that the key to wisdom and contentment is to deny the urges of the flesh to achieve a sense of moderation, or contentment. Taoists believe likewise that the Way is not based on the focus on self, but to break from the momentary urges of the flesh, the momentary fears that dominate—that is, to break away from time.

These philosophies, and Christianity as well, focus on the constraint of time on one's being. They teach that the key to enlightenment, peace, salvation, is to break from the moment, to leave the focus of the present behind and to try to reach an understanding of what transcends the present. If one is constantly focused on how one feels now, or what one wants to achieve now, then one will not realize the truths, the constancy, that transcend the moment. How does one find the transcendent truth of which the moment is just a fleeting part?

If I feel love, moment by moment, and it freezes, then I feel unchanging Love; if I feel life, moment by moment, and it freezes (death), then I feel Life. Death is the point of rest, being still, non-movement, which is so foreign to us, who are constantly in movement, that it is terrifying.

Even Jesus was afraid to die. He sweated blood, such was his anxiety, at the Garden of Gethsemane, according to Luke. He requested that God not make him drink from the cup of death. At the same time, the theme of the Gospels is that Jesus was from the beginning the Messiah, the Logos, the Son of Man, God's Chosen One; that he knew, and predicted over and over, that he was to be arrested, scourged, and crucified. Yet he was still afraid. The philosophy of Christianity is that Jesus was God who became man. The Virgin Birth means that Mary's womb was untouched by time; for pleasure exists in time. Mary's womb was a timeless, singular moment. God existed in the womb as a single moment then became flesh, became time. God willingly took on human flesh, and experienced time. Jesus qua God then spent his life experiencing all that humans experience—the wages of sin, according to the *Book of Genesis*. The sum of Christian thought is that Jesus died for our sins. Precisely how? First, he lived in time, which is the same as sin, then he died, died to time, died to sin. The single moment (God) became a series of moments (Jesus) then returned to the single moment on the Cross and in the Tomb. Likewise, humans come from the single moment that we do not recall and will go to a single moment we cannot anticipate. Jesus, the Logos, the Son of Man, is our guide.

Jesus is the *mediator* in the sense of mediation of momentary time and transcendent time, movement and stillness. Life reveals fleeting moments of the timeless, the stillness. Jesus used earthly concepts and actions that represented this stillness: kingdom, love, peace, healing, completeness. His body and blood, his teachings, connect humans to the state of non-movement, but insufficiently, because everything a human does is based on movement, and a human cannot be *still*, hence know. *Logos* is still. Jesus's healing is temporary, but the way he healed, by love and empathy, is proof of his connection to the eternal, the still.

The final present moment becomes the never-ending moment through love. The experience of love is the way to the transcendent. Love means that a human does not have to ignore the moment, or conquer time, but rather embrace it, embrace time. Time can be the pathway to love. Love can overwhelm the pain, doubt, anger, lust, desire, and hatred. But how, precisely?

Caussade says that the key to entering the divine in each moment is surrender to God's will—*abandonment to divine providence*. God's will is supreme in each moment; this will is love; to resist brings anguish. Hence, one must in each and every moment accept God's will. This is how one embraces God's love to find peace in the moment. The burden of time is the burden not of always trying to escape the moment, to transcend it; it is the burden of finding in the moment peace, life, and love. The burden of time, the burden of the cross, is to find the means to surrender totally to the will of God. This is how to prepare for death, when time is still.

In each moment there are infinite possibilities, infinite relationships. Life is countless people each with an infinite number of potential experiences all interacting and being experienced simultaneously. God in a single moment peruses the whole of experience, the infinite plethora of human experience. God's perusal is empathetic; God feels all these human experiences. This is the role of the Son of Man. Empathy in the singular moment connects with transcendence of human experience. When Mary pondered in her heart she experienced this empathetic transcendence, feeling and sensing the manifold experiences that her child would enjoy and endure over his life. This empathetic transcendence occurs in a single moment of awareness. In this single moment of experience is the entrance to the transcendent truth that is God, as Caussade argued. Isolated human experiences combine into a whole (symbolized by the Son of Man), a united human experience that transcends the individual moment.

Jesus claimed as much when he told the Jews, in the Gospel of John, "I am." He is a transcendent being that existed from the beginning. He *knows*. He is the truth in that he encompasses the inquiries of all individual knowers. Such inquiries are historical inquiries, attempts to reconcile self with time and eternity, that is, the past (self) with time and eternity. If Jesus *is* throughout all lives, if he *is* in all times, then he transcends time, the past. The past does not overwhelm or dominate him because he is content with the present—*he is*. He sums the scattered moments that represent time, the past; he sums all pasts as the son of man, the son of time, the son of history. He is the offspring of time, human actions, human history. He is human history because he encompasses the entire human experience. The past comes to a head, is summoned, in his life. In dying he dies for the sum of human pasts; in living again he shows that the human past can be overcome and that the eternal present, and the escape from the ignorance and limitations of the past, can be accomplished. Each human is plagued by his/her past; it dominates and overwhelms the present, because no one is ever sure, ever comfortable, with the countless choices one has made amid the infinite choices possible. A person makes a choice in time in anticipation of the future, then the future becomes the present and the burden of the choice becomes apparent. A person made the choice out of ignorance of the future and its consequences and must live with the choice.

But Jesus is the "I am," meaning he sees all infinite possibilities in the present based on memory and anticipation. By encompassing all pasts and visualizing all futures in the constant unending moments, he becomes each person, as the Son of Man, living in each, transcending time. To accept Christ is to accept the past, accept the choices amid the infinite, and know that it was and is and will be best. Yes, living in time means a person is ignorant, uncertain, and guilty, but Jesus transcends all these experiences, uncertainties, guilt. A person's actions are their own, their will is free, but by accepting the past, accepting the Son of Man, a person finds redemption and is freed from the burden of the past. Jesus himself accepted his past and transcended it. So too can all humans.

Christ allows each person to say, "I am." All human experience comes to a head in each person—all the good and bad. Each person is responsible in a sense for all human experience. Yet in each and every moment a person has the ability to transcend it all, to know what is right and true. And this is by accepting it, and not struggling against it. By accepting it, a person accepts the past of all humankind, accepts time, accepts sin, accepts ignorance. By accepting a person transcends. By begging forgiveness collectively humans accept and break from the burden of guilt, personal as well as collective guilt. To accept is to stop resisting: To stop replaying in one's mind, to simply accept that "I am"— I simply exist, and this is enough.

This acceptance is the closest a person comes at any one moment to Jesus, who simply *is*. For to experience being in the singular moment is to simply be, to transcend the burden of the past and future, hence to transcend time. To accept is to be. To accept is to find the truth at each moment—to experience the singularity that Jesus represents.

To accept life, this basic gift God has given, is to accept God Himself. If life as it is in the moment is insufficient, then God is deemed insufficient. To be righteous and to enter into the kingdom of God is to accept the moment for what it is, accept God for what He is. To accept the moment is to accept what one has, where one lives, what one does, what one eats, the clothing one wears, the shelter covering one's head. Otherwise it is never sufficient, never enough, the kingdom of God passes by, and a person surrenders to evil.

20

THE GOSPEL OF THE ABSURD

The foolishness of God is wiser than men, and the weakness of God is stronger than men . . .

It was a time of the absurd. All of the systems of thought, the explanations, the examples, the stories—all were absurd. Absurd because they did not make sense. Nevertheless they were compellingly real. They hinted at truth, hiding behind the absurd. Perhaps truth is just on the other side of absurd. The rational type eschews what cannot be seen and known for sure. The atheist is not a fool. Only fools believe what is stated therein. May God bless the atheist. God blesses the fool.

The apparent absurdity of many of the accounts in the Gospels led skeptics of the nineteenth century to try to iron out the wrinkles in the stories, which they could do only by arguing that much of the narrative of the four Gospels appears contrived, written long after the fact, introducing accounts to strengthen a growing Christian movement, to support various interpretations of Christ and his significance. Some skeptics went so far as to write off the entire Passion of Christ as a story, nothing more. How, indeed, can we account for the varying accounts of the *passion*? Are there different versions because of different eyewitnesses, different memories when written down after the fact, different attempts to make it more compelling (Luke) or to fit Jesus into a particular interpretation (John)? Were the accounts written down so long after the fact that stories that had been passed around, that had become almost mythical, were added to the Gospel accounts to make them appear factual? Such was the style of writing and selection of evidence for many biographers and historians writing in the Greco-Roman world of the first century, *Anno Domini*.

Many Christians believe it is consistent to combine reason with faith—reason applied to the Gospels leads a person to seek rational answers to questions of absurdity and contradiction. A person might decide that indeed, the Gospel has stories, not all of them factual, and though doubting the literal truth of the Bible, faith suggests that the stories must be accepted anyway, at least for purposes of membership in the Christian church. Suspending reason for faith is best, because after all, reason is insufficient to explain how a man can be resurrected from the dead. Yet in a world growing more focused on facts and the evidence of the senses, it is quite difficult to build one's entire life on stories from two thousand years ago.

In today's day and age of skepticism and incredulity, it is hard to find serious examples of the transcendent entering time, of *metamorphosis*. Such occurrences exist and are not limited just to humans, but to all life forms. Such metamorphoses have to be sought after, thought about, reflected upon, before they are realized for what they are.

Paul, after his conversion on the road to Damascus, knew that there were many others like him who had been skeptical about the stories of Jesus the healer and redeemer, the Christ. But in an instant he had gone from being a doubter to a believer.

So somehow or another he had to convince others who might not have gone through the same dramatic metamorphosis. How to do it? How to convince skeptical, reasonable people who had been taught that Scripture would be fulfilled in a certain way that it had been fulfilled in quite an unexpected, even absurd way? Paul decided that the absurdity of it all was the key. It was absurd that he, a good rational Pharisee, was all of the sudden transformed, his world turned upside down, to become a believer in something he would have typically doubted, to become someone who would risk anything to bring such a belief to others, who would be whipped, stoned, beaten, cursed, over and over, and yet he was compelled to keep going. Paul came to empty himself, becoming a slave to Christ. The whole thing was crazy, absurd. And yet he had to, for he knew the truth. And strangely, knowing the truth set him free from fear and doubt.

So Paul began to preach and write, and to use reason whenever he could, to use logical arguments, using Scripture and history to convince others that Jesus was the Christ. But within his argument, at a core level in his teaching, was the realization that some of what he taught bordered on the absurd. For example, when he wrote to the Philippians he noted the absurdity that the savior of world would appear as a slave, and so humble himself to be abused in every way possible, and to do it willingly. Paul summed up his theory in his first letter to the Corinthians, when he wrote that "the foolishness of God is wiser than men, and the weakness of God is stronger than men."

Paul was brilliant in his assessment of God's folly and its meaning for humans. The entire incarnation brings about incredulity because it seems so absurd: virgin birth, God becoming man, angels and shepherds, magi worshiping baby, obscure healer and carpenter who is God, God allowing himself to be crucified, resurrection of a dead human body. Jesus's parables seem to indicate his awareness of the folly of his role in life, trying to teach people about eternity who are wrapped up in the fears of the present. He seems incredulous at times about his role and purpose, though he is driven to it. He seems relieved when he is finally arrested, crucified, and dies, as the folly of his life comes to an end. God's folly is truth and wisdom to us. How can it not be, for God to experience time, sin, ignorance, pain, for God to be around us humans so limited in perspective and wisdom?

In some respects the story of Jesus's life, death, and crucifixion is the Gospel of the *absurd*. Jesus is referred to as the lamb of God, a sacrificial atonement for sin: the Jewish passover lamb is a human; Jesus suggests that a person eat his body as bread, and drink his blood as wine; Jesus and the Roman Procurator Pontius Pilate engage in a dialogue discussing the nature of truth before Pilate condemns Jesus to a horrible death; Judas betrays Jesus with a kiss; Jesus's most loyal follower Peter denies him three times—and of course there are many more examples of miracles, healings, and contradictions found in the four Gospels.

The absurdity of the entrance of God into time, the experience of metamorphosis, is not restricted to the accounts of Jesus and his disciples; rather, the Son of Man works through all humans, all existence, over time.

21

PERFECT LOVE

There is no fear in love. But perfect love drives out fear.

John, in his *First Epistle*, wrote that love knows no fear, but John and his fellow disciples, and many others before and since, have feared love. People feared Jesus's love because it was love based in the moment not the transcendent. It is grand to conceive of a distant, universal love, present if out of reach, existent if distant, timeless if impossible to access in time. Jesus was, however, completely a part of time, he lived in time, he was born, lived, died. He experienced time, formed history, saw himself in terms of the past, present, and future, saw himself in human time, human history. Truth is not found in death, rather in life. Truth is not found in the timeless, rather in time. Truth is found in passing moments. The ability to transcend the moments, to put them together, to see what they mean, is to find truth. The moment one is born, the moment one dies, are still moments, like each and every moment. One begins and ends in time. Hence time and its passing are incredibly important for an understanding of what is truth and its meaning for each person.

Each moment is an entrance into the divine. Each moment a

person experiences something that transcends time, that unites all humans throughout time. Behavior such as hatred, violence, avarice, and selfishness detach a person from the experiences that unite, bond humans together in time. Such is the meaning of love, which is the link to all human endeavor, to all life. Love is the transcendent force that links individuals, links all humanity, links all life, in a mystical way. No person is self-fulfilling. Every human has the same feelings, the same emotions, the same ultimate aims: comfort, happiness, security, contentment, all of which are found not singularly, rather collectively. God represents that collectivity. God represents the transcendent, those feelings of comfort, happiness, security, and contentment that humans seek moment by moment. Humans seek love in each moment. Love is found in each moment, found in all moments. God is found in each moment, found in all moments. Since humans are aware only in the present, a person is aware only of what is known in the moment, aware only of love now in the moment, aware only of God *now*. But there are unending distractions from this love, this feeling that can be sensed each moment. The key to happiness is to be aware of the love present in each moment, and not be torn from it, not be distracted by fear to where it cannot be experienced. Love is the living water flowing from the past into the present and future.

The truth that sets us free in each and every moment is love. We just have to be aware of it. We have to break, like Legion did, from distractions that keep us from it. Power, wealth, hatred, hurting others, rejecting others, selfishness, are distractions that keep us from this love, hence they are things of a moment that vanish. Upon death we will not retain power or wealth—but we will retain love.

Who am I but a fool to disregard the *truth*? Jesus preached, represented, Love: to live appropriately is to love. Love is the universal, the basis for all things. Only a society based on pure and utter love will work. Jesus loved all, even sinners. All he asks is that we love. He will love us regardless. If I love I will unite with God, enjoy eternal happiness (that is, eternal love). If I reject Love, do not love, I will experience emptiness and sorrow. Free will means some people might reject love notwithstanding all the opportunities to experience and to accept it. To accept Jesus is to accept love: God knows who are the ones who love. He will one day be, and even now is, embracing such people in Love.

Legion experienced the healing love of Christ in the moment. Mark and Luke tell the story in their typical fashion of ignoring the duration of time, so that it is difficult to determine if the metamorphosis of Legion happened in a second, a minute, a few hours, or a few days.

Unlike others, who would scarcely approach such a man of strength and savagery, an insane, almost inhuman force haunting tombs, Jesus not only came toward the man, but spoke to him. He recognized the man as a man, not a savage, an animal, or a lunatic. He saw that Legion was not a threat, rather was a person who needed compassion, understanding, healing. Jesus knew all about temptation and deception, about the power of what could be, what could have been, what might be, what might have been. Images of the past and future haunt, confuse, sow doubt, mystify, so that reality and fantasy are scarcely distinguishable, and memory is clouded by a mixture of what was with what could have been. The actual events of Legion's past are unknown to us, were unknown to Jesus, perhaps were even unknown to Legion himself. They were like massive rumbling waves, constant and irresistible, overwhelming the shores of the present, crashing in with the unstoppable force of the past. To lessen the waves, to reduce their impact, to calm the sea, required a person of such compassion, such empathy, such understanding and love—only one such person has ever existed, and this was the man whom Legion was fortunate to meet.

Somehow or other, Jesus took upon himself Legion's fears, insecurities, memories, past, and sin, and through love and empathy broke the weight of the past to make the present endurable and the future possible. Demons coming out of people such as Legion are released by the person himself. The legion of fear within *is allowed to be there*. When finding someone through whom to release it, it is voluntarily released. A person cries out, you are the Son of God, because the demons of time feed on momentary fears and desires, and then they see someone who is timeless, that is, who represents the transcendent, and such truth pulls, as it were, the demon time from within the person. Legion saw in Jesus, in his demeanor, his eyes, his words, that he transcended the momentary, and could therefore be trusted with the burden of the legion of fear.

The disciple Jesus loved, John, knew precisely what happened to Legion, precisely what happens to all people metamorphosized by Jesus's love. "Perfect love drives out fear," John wrote in his *First Epistle*, "because fear has to do with punishment." The Greek word John used for punishment, *kŏlasis* (κόλασις), translates as *infliction*. Punishment is infliction, something inflicted—inflicted by the self. *Fear is self-inflicted*. Perfect love knows no self-inflicted fear. Perfect love is unencumbered by time. When Jesus healed Legion, he was able to remove the vestiges of fear based on a guilt inspired past and uncertain future. Jesus healed Legion from self-inflicted fear. The release from fear is the true metamorphosis.

NOTES

3. The Terror of Nature and the Divine

1. Aeschylus, "Prometheus Bound," trans. Rex Warner, in *Ten Greek Plays in Contemporary Translations* (Boston: Houghton Mifflin Company, 1957).
2. Ibid.
3. James Grahame, *The Sabbath*.
4. Quoted in E. R. Dodds, *Pagan & Christian in an Age of Anxiety* (New York: W. W. Norton and Co., 1970), 44.
5. Quoted in Rudolf Steiner, *Esoteric Christianity: The Gospel of St. John and Ancient Mysteries*, Rudolf Steiner Archive & e.Lib: https://wn.rsarchive.org/Lectures/19061127p01.html
6. Homer, *The Odyssey*, trans. Robert Fitzgerald (New York: Random House, 1990).
7. Philo, *On a Contemplative Life*, vol. 4, trans. C. D. Yonge (London: Bohn, 1855); Marcus Aurelius, *Meditations*, trans. Maxwell Staniforth (Harmondsworth, Middlesex, England: Penguin Books, 1964); Boethius, *The Consolation of Philosophy*. trans. W. V. Cooper (New York: Random House, 1943).

4. An Age of Deception

1. Plutarch, "Of Superstition Or Indiscreet Devotion," trans. William Baxter, in *Essays and Miscellanies*, volume 1 (Boston Little, Brown, and Company, 1905).

5. A Vision of the Night

1. Plutarch, "Rules for the Preservation of Health," trans. Matthew Poole, in *Essays and Miscellanies*, vol. 1.
2. Plutarch, *Of Superstition*.
3. Plutarch, "On God's Slowness to Punish," trans. Robin Waterfield, in *Essays* (London: Penguin Books, 1992).

4. Plutarch, "A Discourse to an Unlearned Prince," trans. J. Kersey, in *Essays and Miscellanies*, vol. 4.
5. Plutarch, "Why the Oracles Cease to Give Answers," trans. Robert Midgley, in *Essays and Miscellanies*, vol. 1.
6. Angels are spirits who serve God (Heb 1,14) and who brought the Law to the Hebrews (Acts 7.53).
7. *Dream (onar)* in the *Gospel of Matthew* comes from a root word that means message or gift.

9. Hidden Years

1. Augustine, *Confessions*, trans R. S. Pine-Coffin (Harmondsworth, Middlesex, England: Penguin Books, 1961).
2. Edward Young, *Night Thoughts, On Life, Death, and Immorality*, revised 3rd ed (London: William Tegg, 1853).
3. Isaac Williams, *The Cathedral* (London: Griffith, Farran, Okeden & Welsh, 1889).
4. Jean-Pierre de Caussade, *Abandonment to Divine Providence*, trans. John Beevers (New York: Doubleday, 1975).
5. Augustine, *Confessions*.

10. Deceiver

1. Isaac Williams, *Cathedral*
2. *Satanas* (as opposed to *Satan*, devil) in Matthew (according to Strong's Dictionary) is Aramaic/Chaldean in origin and means *accuser*. Devil, or *diabolos*, means false accuser, slanderer, traducer (to humiliate or disgrace). Satan is called or referred to in the New Testament as adversary, enemy, accuser, serpent, dragon, author of evil, beguiler of eve, tempter. A synonym of tempter is *seducer*.
3. Mark 8:33, which is comparable to Matthew 4, 10, in which Jesus uses the same verb (Go, *ypage*) and says, "Go, Satan," in response to Satan's tempting in the wilderness.

11. Timeless Enters Time

1. Ovid, *Metamorphoses*, trans. Henry T. Riley (Philadelphia: McKay, 1899).
2. Philo, *On a Contemplative Life*.
3. Apuleius, *Metamorphosis*, trans. Thomas Taylor (London: 1822).

4. Philo, *A Treatise on the Account of the Creation of the World*, trans. C. D. Yonge.
5. Marcus Aurelius, *Meditations*.
6. Ibid. Two hundred years later, the Stoic philosopher and Christian theologian Aurelius Augustine built a sophisticated paean to God in his book *The City of God*.
7. Luke, chapter 9; Mark, chapter 9; Matthew, chapters 16 and 17.

15. Son of Man

1. Elaine Pagels, *The Gnostic Gospels* (New York: Random House, 1981), 147, quoting Irenaeus.
2. William Barclay, *Jesus as They Saw Him* (New York: Harper & Row, 1962), 75.
3. Josephus, *The Jewish War*, trans. G. A. Williamson (Harmondsworth, Middlesex, England: Penguin Books, 1959), 398-399.
4. *The Nag Hammadi Library*, ed. James Robinson (New York: HarperCollins Publishers, 1990).

16. Truth

1. *The New Oxford Annotated Bible with Apocrypha*, 102.
2. *Wisdom of Solomon*, 3:1-3.

18. The Voice of a Child

1. Augustine, *Confessions*.
2. Montaigne, "Of Experience," in *Essays*, trans. Donald Frame.

SOURCES CONSULTED

Bible Translations

The Bible: Authorized King James Version with Apocrypha. *Oxford: Oxford University Press, 1997.*

The Five Gospels: What did Jesus Really Say? The Search for the Authentic Words of Jesus. *Edited by Robert W. Funk. New York: HarperCollins, 1996.*

The Interlinear NIV: Parallel New Testament in Greek and English. *Translated by Alfred Marshall. Grand Rapids, MI: Zondervan Publishing House, 1976.*

The New Jerusalem Bible: The Complete Text of the Ancient Canon of the Scriptures. *Standard Edition. New York: Random House, 1999.*

The New Oxford Annotated Bible with the

Apocrypha. *Revised Standard Version.* New York: Oxford University Press, 1977.

Powell, J. Enoch. The Evolution of the Gospel: A New Translation of the First Gospel with Commentary and Introductory Essay. *Yale, CT: Yale University Press, 1994.*

Contemporary Sources

Aeschylus. "Prometheus Bound." *Translated by Rex Warner. In* Ten Greek Plays in Contemporary Translations. *Boston: Houghton Mifflin Company, 1957.*

Apuleius. The Metamorphosis, or Golden Ass, and Philosophical Works, of Apuleius. *Translated by Thomas Taylor. London: Robert Triphook, 1822.*

Aristotle. "On Prophesying by Dreams." *In* The Works of Aristotle. *Volume 1. Chicago: Encyclopedia Britannica, Inc., 1952.*

Boethius, The Consolation of Philosophy. *Translated by W. V. Cooper. New York: Random House, 1943.*

Diogenes Laertius. Lives of the Eminent Philosophers. *Two volumes. Translated by R. D. Hicks. Cambridge: Harvard University Press, 1925.*

Early Greek Philosophy. *Translated by Jonathan Barnes. New York: Penguin Books, 1987.*

Herodotus. The Histories. *Translated by Aubrey de Selincourt. Harmondsworth, Middlesex, England: Penguin Books, 1972.*

Hesiod. Works and Days, Theogony and The Shield of Heracles. *Translated by Hugh G. Evelyn-White. Mineola, NY: Dover Publications, 2006.*

Homer. The Iliad. *Translated by Robert Fitzgerald. New York: Anchor Books, 1974.*

Homer. The Odyssey. *Translated by Robert Fitzgerald. New York: Random House, 1990.*

Josephus. The Jewish War. *Translated by G. A. Williamson. Harmondsworth, Middlesex, England: Penguin Books, 1959.*

Marcus Aurelius. Meditations. *Translated by Maxwell Staniforth. Harmondsworth, Middlesex, England: Penguin Books, 1964.*

Ovid. The Metamorphoses of Ovid. *Translated by Henry T. Riley. Philadelphia: David McKay, 1899.*

Philo Judaeus. The Works of Philo Judaeus. Volume 4. *Translated by C. D. Yonge. London: Henry G. Bohn, 1855.*

Pliny the Elder. Natural History: A Selection. *Translated by James F. Healy. London: Penguin Books, 1991.*

Plutarch. Essays. *Translated by Robin Waterfield. London: Penguin Books, 1992.*

Plutarch. Essays and Miscellanies. *Corrected and Revised by William W. Goodwin. Volumes One, Three, and Four. Boston: Little, Brown, and Company, 1905, 1906, 1909.*

Saint Augustine. City of God. *Translated by Henry Bettenson. London: Penguin Books, 1984.*

Saint Augustine. Confessions. *Translated by R. S. Pine-Coffin. Harmondsworth, Middlesex, England: Penguin Books, 1961.*

The Epic of Gilgamesh. *Translated by N. K. Sandars. London: Penguin Books, 1972.*

The Nag Hammadi Library. *James M. Robinson, General Editor. New York: HarperCollins Publishers, 1990.*

Secondary Sources

Barclay, William. Jesus as They Saw Him. *New York: Harper & Row, 1962.*

Beavis, Mary Ann and Michael J. Gilmour. Dictionary of the Bible and Western Culture. *Sheffield, UK: Sheffield Phoenix Press, 2012.*

Caussade, Jean-Pierre de. Abandonment to Divine

Providence. *Translated by John Beevers. New York: Doubleday, 1975.*

Dodds, E. R. Pagan & Christian in an Age of Anxiety. *New York: W. W. Norton and Co., 1970.*

Grahame, James. "The Sabbath." *In* The Works of the British Poets, Selected and Chronologically Arranged. *Volume 3. New York: D. Appleton & Company, 1856.*

Grant, Michael. Jesus: An Historian's Review of the Gospels. *New York: Charles Sribner's Sons, 1977.*

Hobbes, Thomas. Leviathan. *In* Selections. *Edited by Frederick J. E. Woodbridge. New York: Charles Scribner's Sons, 1958.*

Lamberton, Robert. Plutarch. *New Haven, CT: Yale University Press, 2001.*

Montaigne, Michel de. The Complete Essays of Montaigne. *Translated by Donald M. Frame. Stanford: Stanford University Press, 1958.*

Pagels, Elaine. The Gnostic Gospels. *New York, Random House, 1981.*

Steiner, Rudolf. Esoteric Christianity: The Gospel of St. John and Ancient Mysteries. *Rudolf Steiner Archive & e.Lib:*
https://wn.rsarchive.org/Lectures/19061127p01.html

Strong, James. *The New Strong's Complete Dictionary of Bible Words. Nashville, TN: Thomas Nelson Publishers, 1996.*

Wilcox, Donald J. *The Measure of Time's Past: Pre-Newtonian Chronologies and the Rhetoric of Relative Time. Chicago: University of Chicago Press, 1987.*

Williams, Isaac. *The Cathedral, Or the Catholic and Apostolic Church in England. London: Griffith, Farran, Okeden & Welsh, 1889.*

Young, Edward. *Night Thoughts, On Life, Death, and Immorality. Revised 3rd edition. London: William Tegg, 1853.*

ABOUT THE AUTHOR

Russell M. Lawson was born and raised in Tulsa, Oklahoma. His first intellectual interest was in ancient Greek mythology, which led to a lifelong fascination with the history of the ancient Mediterranean. He matriculated at Oklahoma State University from 1975 to 1979, majoring in history. From 1980 to 1982, he studied at OSU for a Master's degree in Ancient Mediterranean history. He earned a Ph.D. in American history from the University of New Hampshire in 1987. He has taught at schools in New England, Oklahoma, and Ontario. Dr. Lawson teaches and writes on the history of ideas. He has written eighteen books: nonfiction, fiction, reference. He is married, has three sons, and four rescue pups.

www.ingramcontent.com/pod-product-compliance
Lightning Source LLC
Chambersburg PA
CBHW062027220426
43662CB00010B/1506